3 4143 00652 1429

JUST ASK
the right questions to
get what you want

ɔckt<

D0334707

11

This book is dedicated to the memory of

'The two mums'
Stella and Renée...

'It'll be lucky to you!'

JUST ASK
the right questions to
get what you want

Ian Cooper

WARRINGTON BOROUGH COUNCIL	
Askews	21-Jun-2007

PEARSON

Prentice Hall

LIFE

Pearson Education Limited
Edinburgh Gate
Harlow
Essex CM20 2JE
England

© Ian Cooper 2007

First published 2007

The right of Ian Cooper to be identified as author of this Work has been
asserted by him in accordance with the Copyright, Designs and Patents
Act, 1988.

All rights reserved. No part of this publication may be reproduced,
stored in a retrieval system or transmitted in any form or by any means
electronic, mechanical, photocopying, recording, or otherwise, without
either the prior written permission of the publishers and copyright
owners or a licence permitting restricted copying in the United Kingdom
issued by the Copyright Licensing Agency Ltd., 90 Tottenham Court
Road, London W1T 4LP.

ISBN 978-0-273-71278-7

Commissioning Editor: Emma Shackleton
Project Editor: Cheryl Lanyon
Designer: Kevin O'Connor
Cover Design: Annette Peppis
Senior Production Controller: Man Fai Lau

Printed and bound by Henry Ling, UK

The Publisher's policy is to use paper manufactured from sustainable
forests.

Who is Ian Cooper?

Having worked previously as a lecturer, freelance author and journalist, Ian has spent the last 22 years as a business and personal development consultant and skills presenter. He is one of Europe's most experienced communications advisers to both professional practices and service industry organizations. IIe is particularly known for his lively, down-to-earth, practical and entertaining seminars, and has clocked up more than 5,000 speaking engagements, both in-house and at public venues. Using many of the question techniques in this book he has helped thousands of people find solutions to their personal and business problems, and has often been the catalyst for change and for making things happen.

He has been married for 30 years and has three grown-up children and a dog. In his spare time he acts with a local amateur dramatic group.

A note to readers from Ian

If anyone has a comment or success story about the use of questions or would simply like to 'Just Ask' Ian Cooper a question he can be contacted via e mail at: justaskian@yahoo.com

Acknowledgements

First of all my gratitude and thanks to all those friends, relatives, clients, seminar delegates, members of the public and bloody-minded 'jobsworths' who don't even know that they need thanking, for the inspiration for many of the situations and examples in this book!

Although I am the one who has physically sat at the computer for hours at times of the day I had forgotten about, you wouldn't be reading this now had it not been for the vision, encouragement and guidance of my literary agent Peter Knight and my Commissioning Editor, Emma Shackleton. My grateful thanks to them.

To my talented offspring, Samantha, Howard and David, my thanks for the inspiration behind many of the ideas in this book.

However, the 'Oscar' for Best Supporting Role must go to my wife Helene. She has put up with my questions for 30 years and has been a constant source of love and encouragement. As regards this book, she has provided me with ideas, inspiration, wisdom over what to leave out when my warped sense of humour began to get the better of me, allowed me to feature her in many examples and has been the ultimate 'apostrophe hunter'. What husband could ask for more?

Contents

The 'Technology of Questions™'   54

Contents

Questions to 'just ask' yourself   116

Life situations: the questions to 'just ask...'   146

The power of questions – it's all yours   178

'WHAT?' is the meaning of life

Since time began, mankind has regarded the question 'What is the meaning of life?' as the ultimate question. Enter it into an internet search engine and you could spend the next few years aimlessly browsing through more than 243 million possibilities.

The planet's greatest thinkers, philosophers, quantum physicists, scientists, authors, theologians and 'gurus' of all ages, shapes, sizes and denominations have wrestled unsuccessfully with this question. Douglas Adams tells us in his science fiction series that the ultimate answer to life, the universe and everything is '42', and even the Monty Python comedy team made a full-length feature film about the question.

Yet, despite all this, for the first time ever, here and now in this humble little book, I am going to solve this eternal mystery for you. The truth is that the answer actually lies in the question!

WHAT?... is the meaning of life!

Yes, read it again and keep reading it until you get it.
It is, in fact, a statement and *not* a question.

WHAT?... is the answer!

Let me explain what I mean.

Since the earliest times, human beings have sought to achieve, grow, develop, innovate, inspire, explore, learn, understand, create, imagine, discover, invent, find, challenge and improve. When I say that **'What?'** *is* the meaning of life, this is because I am regarding the word 'What?' as a metaphor for the innate questioning process that has driven mankind to achieve everything it has on both a collective and a personal level.

When we personally seek answers to our trivial domestic and business issues, when governments strive for international solutions to world problems, and when scientists look for cures for illness and disease, all are essentially doing no more than asking questions. Can you think of one single, man made, historical, cultural or technological event, achievement or even tragedy that didn't happen because someone, somewhere asked a question?

Consider various aspects of life and you'll see how important questions are:

The medical world: We have drugs, treatments and surgical innovations today that keep people alive and well, when years ago they would have died. Why? Because scientists and doctors have constantly asked questions such as 'What causes that?' and 'How do we solve that problem?' On a more personal level, how do your doctors diagnose your problems? They ask you questions and then they ask themselves questions, such as 'What does that mean?'

The legal system: Our systems of law and order are driven by questions concerning our personal freedoms, our safety and security, and justice and fair play. What is the main tool used by our law-enforcement agencies, the courts and the legal profession to get to the truth? Questions!

The world of business: This revolves around questions such as 'How do we maximize revenue whilst minimizing expenses?' and 'How do we get an advantage over our competitors?'

Religion: Every religion in the world has as its main focus the questions 'What do we believe?', 'How do we get closer to the divine?', and 'How can we reflect our beliefs in our daily practices?'

Think also of those who work in teaching, entertainment, exploration, science, technology and the creative arts. Every single one of them is driven by questions to advance their thinking and to help them come up with something new.

On an incredibly mundane level, isn't it the case that your first thoughts as you open your eyes every day are, in fact, questions? 'What day is it?', 'What am I doing today?', 'How do I feel?', 'Can I be bothered to get out of bed?', 'What am I going to have for breakfast?'

Isn't it a fact that it is the questions you have asked at various points in your life that have brought you to where you are now in every respect? Think about some of the questions you've asked yourself, or others, over the years and their influence over who you are today and the life that you lead:

- ? Who do I want as friends?
- ? What subjects shall I choose to study?
- ? What do I want to be when I grow up?
- ? Where do I want to live?
- ? Do I want to marry? Who do I want to marry? Will you marry me?
- ? Shall we have children? What shall we call them?

? What do I believe?
? How can I help?
? Shall I change jobs?
? Shall I buy this book about 'just asking'? Shall I read it?

So, why is all this important in the context of this book? Because, once you realize that 'just asking' questions is the single most important factor in determining what will happen to you in the future, you will appreciate how and why mastering the 'question process' will give you a level of influence and control over getting whatever you want.

The problem for many people is that they spend their entire life seeking answers without really understanding that, in order to find them, they need to ask the right questions.

So, next time you hear the question, 'What is the meaning of life?' all you have to do is to smile and respond with:

Yes, you're right!

So, what do you need to know?

The decisions we take in life, and the results that flow from these decisions, are influenced by the questions we ask. Therefore, the quality of those questions affects our decisions and their ultimate outcome.

Ask more and better questions, and more often you will get better results!

Introduction

Do you know what holds you back more than anything else? Well, let me tell you bluntly now. It is your failure to ASK for what you want!

If I pushed you into instantly telling me the things you wanted to achieve and improve in your business, career or personal life, your mind would initially go blank. Eventually, however, you would come up with a whole shopping list of 'wants' and aspirations. Once we get rid of the flippant sports cars, sun-baked beaches and digital, plasma, turbo-powered televisions; and the more general, 'I just want world peace and to make the world a better place', the likelihood is that you'd wish for some, or all, of the following:

◆ for your existing customers or clients to buy more from you;
◆ to feel able to increase your prices or fees;
◆ to get a better deal on the goods or services you are thinking of buying;
◆ a promotion, salary increase, more responsibility (or all three!);
◆ to take someone out and develop a relationship with them, for business or personal reasons;
◆ if you are self-employed, for time to do other things and for the chance to sell out at some stage in return for a decent pot of cash!;
◆ to be fitter, healthier and, if you have medical problems, to find a quick and painless solution to them.

I have good news for you. I can guarantee you right now, before you go any further with your reading, that there is a two-word instruction that, if followed, can immediately bring you closer to success with all of these desires. These two words are the 'holy grail' of personal and business success. The problem is that they appear so obvious, clichéd, personally challenging, embarrassing or uncomfortable, that they are often ignored, forgotten or deliberately avoided for fear of rejection.

So, here, then, are the two words that can change your life:

Just ask!

That's it!

Everything after this is mere detail, technique and a way of thinking, and these things are what the rest of this book is about. So you are faced with a choice: are you going to stop now, having learned the ingredients for success; or are you going to read the rest of the book to find out how to make them work?

Remember, if there is something you want, just ask for it outright.

'Surely, it can't be that simple?' you're thinking to yourself. But how do you know? I mean how do you *really* know? Have you tried it out?

Let me ask you some blunt questions:

? When did you last ask a customer outright to buy more from you? And by that I don't mean simply sending them a carefully and cleverly worded letter, casually mentioning various other services in the hope that they will rush to spend their money with you. I mean when did you last, very specifically, ask an existing customer to buy more from you?

? When did you last ask your customers or clients to pay more for your various goods or services? Also let me ask you something else: what percentage of your customer or client base complains about your charges and then stops buying from you? If it is less than 10 per cent, you are not charging enough. Think about it!

? Imagine you are buying something in a shop, booking a hotel or engaging someone to perform a service for you. When was the last time you bluntly asked for a better deal?

? Do you want a pay rise, or a promotion, or more responsibility? Have you ever gone in to your boss and asked for it outright?

? Suppose you want to meet someone, either for personal or business reasons. What do you do? I know many people who have gone to great lengths to contrive to meet someone, only to find limited opportunities to talk because of the constraints of time, place or good taste. Why not just pick up the phone and ask that person to meet you?

? If you have some health-related problem, have you ever asked for a second opinion? Have you asked about alternative remedies? When did you last ask your doctor to review your cocktail of pills and medications?

The truth is, most people have rarely considered these questions and asked outright for these things. If you have, then you will know there are only three possible replies:

Yes! Maybe! No!

Although I confess to you now that you are never going to succeed 100 per cent of the time, in order to maximize the chances of getting a 'yes', turning a 'maybe' into a 'yes' or converting the 'nos' into something more positive, you need to know exactly *how* to ask in order to get the outcome you want. That is what this book is all about. Of course, I also recognize that simply blurting out your innermost desires, as Aladdin did whilst rubbing his lamp, is not the answer. You need to be respectful, courteous, thoughtful and sensible if you are going to be successful at 'just asking'. At the very least, say please!

By the end of this book you will have unconsciously absorbed the **'Just Asking' mindset**, understood the **Golden Rules of 'Just Asking'** and been introduced to the **'Technology of Questions™'**. These are a combination of simple, common-sense tips and linguistic techniques, which anyone can learn and master very quickly. They have all been tried and tested successfully by myself and others many times, and over the last 20 years I have trained thousands of business and professional people in how to use them. You, too, will be able to access and use all these techniques.

I am also going to give you a whole set of **Questions to 'Just Ask' Yourself**. This section acknowledges that getting what you want is not always measured in terms of financial, business and career success. By asking yourself appropriate questions so that your mind is forced to focus on certain personal issues, there are many ways in which you can enhance the quality of your life and improve your personal performance in a whole host of areas.

In addition, you will also find a section on various **Life Situations** where 'just asking' is hugely important. These cover making decisions, getting medical help, making conversation, making better deals and complaining when that becomes necessary.

THE GOLDEN RULES OF 'JUST ASKING'

Before we get to the techniques, or the
'Technology of Questions™' as I like to call
them, I want to give you what I regard as the
Golden Rules of 'Just Asking'. These are
more a way of thinking than anything else. I
want you to understand these first, so that,
when I give you the techniques, you will be
positively 'lusting' for them, but will also be in
the right psychological state to receive them,
believe in them and use them successfully in
your various enterprises and endeavours.

Be blunt and ask openly

As I mentioned in the introduction, the majority of people simply don't ask for what they want, with the hardly surprising result that they don't get it. The first rule is to know that:

You can and should ask bluntly and openly in the most appropriate and respectful way.

In fact, make it a must! You are denying yourself massive opportunities, potential success and happiness if you don't.

Asking puts *you* in the driving seat of your destiny.

Your future is shaped by your willingness to ask the upfront questions that perhaps other people either don't think of, or are too afraid to ask. From a practical point of view, your first and most important step is to make the mental commitment and resolve to ask for what you want. You may not know initially *how* you are going to ask, but don't let that put you off! The 'how' is a detail.

Here's the deal: *you* make the commitment to ask and *I'll* give you a book full of 'hows'.

Remember, the moment you do ask, you dramatically increase the odds in your favour.

Some years ago I was contacted by a commercial organization that had been trying to market a particular specialist service to financial institutions for some time. They had advertised in trade publications, attended exhibitions, written standard mailshots – all without any real success. As far as they were concerned they had drawn a blank, and they wanted my suggestions. I disappointed them ... I only had one.

I told them to ask their targets outright exactly what they would have to do in order to interest them in the particular service they wanted to sell.

After a lot of discussion about this, the client concluded this wasn't high-powered or high-tech enough for them, that they weren't comfortable doing this, didn't know how and, anyway. 'it wasn't really appropriate'. I was sent on my way.

A year later they invited me along again and told me that, after a further year's expenditure on advertising and trade shows, they still hadn't made any serious progress and wondered if I would be prepared to do the asking for them that I had suggested the previous year. I agreed.

Here is what happened in general terms. Having identified exactly which financial institutions my client most wanted, and to whom in those institutions I needed to speak (I found out by asking!), I picked up the phone and very respectfully asked the most outrageously blunt question. I apologized to the relevant person at the outset about the direct and unorthodox approach, confessed that we had been trying unsuccessfully for a while through advertising and mailshots to interest them in our particular services, and then asked if they could help. I asked them, 'What is the best way to get you to consider us, and how do you go about deciding who to use for this kind of service?'

Without boring you with the details of this project, let me just say that I was given the answer, we followed it to the letter and, using many of the rules and techniques in this book, the client has now done over a million pounds' worth of business with that institution.

Afterwards, the grateful and impressed client wanted to know how I had performed this miraculous feat. Without thinking about it too seriously, I replied, 'Well, I did what I said I was going to do. I just asked them how to do it, and they told me.'

'Yes,' said the client. 'I know that, but I suspect it is more to do with how you asked!'

He was right, of course. But first I had to have the right mindset. I had to know with total confidence that I could ask, and that I would be respected for asking, provided it was done in a courteous, respectful, professional, honest and understanding manner. I also knew that, because so few ask in this very open and upfront way, I was immediately increasing the odds of success.

What can I do differently?

It is important to realize that sometimes it isn't just the questions we ask others that can have the biggest influence over our lives, but those we ask ourselves. Business and personal consultants will tell you that this is what strategic thinking is all about. I don't disagree – I just want to simplify the idea.

Take a look at my definition of business or personal madness: **Doing today what you did yesterday, and expecting different results!**

Once you understand the power of these words it becomes obvious that, if you want to get a different, indeed better, result, you are going to have to change something. In my business experience, too many organizations and individuals face a real dilemma. They want better results, but they also want to carry on exactly as before. With this in mind, the single most important business and personal question that you should be asking is:

?   **What can I do differently?**

Again, a statement of the obvious, but when was the last time you pointed your mind at a specific business or personal issue that you would like to improve and asked that question? The problem is that so many aspects of what we do are such automatic, standard and routine habits, that we no longer even think to question the way we do them.

> A leading professional practice rang me up one day and said that they often have to write tenders and proposals in direct competition with other firms. They explained they had written 12 of these over the past 18 months, pitching for substantial pieces of business. Unfortunately they had not won any of them. When I asked why they thought this was, their head of marketing confessed that they didn't know and that was why they were calling me.

> I asked them to send me the 12 written proposals and the details of each opportunity. The next day a van arrived and a relieved courier heaved this massive package into my arms. I sat down to read the tenders. The first looked very professional and it made extremely impressive reading. The second, however, was identical to the first in every respect except that the name of the prospect had been changed throughout on a word processor. The third,

fourth, and indeed all the rest, were also exactly the same – word for impressive word!

When I pointed this out to the firm, and asked why they were all the same, they replied,

'Well, the first one was so time-consuming we thought it would be good to use it as a template for all our tenders. We set up a file on our computer system called 'Tenders', which any of our team could tap into. It has really speeded the process up.'

Well, by now I hope you are smiling at this firm's errors. Having created a system for dealing with tenders, they thought that was it. It was all so routine and systemized that getting the tenders out had become more important than what they were for. It's obvious when you stop and think about it. The problem is, too many people don't stop and think, and ask the question **'What can I do differently?'**

Had this firm done so, they would have realized that they have to treat and write each tender individually, according to the unique needs of that prospect. What is staggering is that they had submitted and failed 12 times before they even thought to ask themselves why they had never won!

Always be prepared to ask, what can I do differently?

Have you ever sent out large numbers of letters chasing job vacancies and enclosed your CV? What is your success rate? If it is low, maybe you need to change something?

Don't assume the answer will be 'no'

This is one of the biggest and most common traps. I have heard the following complaint thousands of times:

'There's no point in asking because...

... we've no chance;

... we're too small;

... we're too big;

... we're too expensive;

... we can't compete;

... we're too new in the marketplace;

... we're perceived as too old-fashioned;

... they already have a relationship;

... they won't pay that;

... they'll never come down that far;

... they won't take me seriously;

... I'm too fat;

... I'm too small;

... they'll laugh at me.'

Get the picture? How many more assumptions like these can you come up with, or have you used? However realistic they might seem, they are no more than excuses for your own lack of technique, comfort, or fear about asking the question. As I mentioned before, the one thing I can guarantee you is that, if you don't ask, you will certainly not get what you want. I can tell you now that, by ignoring what appeared to be realistic and rationally valid assumptions, I have asked:

? **for millions of pounds' worth of business for clients who said they stood no chance;**

? **for substantial charitable donations from people whom you would expect to say 'no';**

? **for joint ventures for clients with business partners who would regard themselves as being in a much higher league;**

? **for celebrities I have never met to agree to help with various projects for no payment.**

And got them all!

If that doesn't convince you, I have even got the car parking attendant at my local city railway station to let me in and find me a parking place when the car park sign read 'FULL', while other cars drove away *assuming* there were no places!

How?

I asked! I'll tell you what I said later. In the meantime, remember this:

To assume makes an *ass* out of *u* and *me!*

Assumptions are the enemy of success!

What's the worst that can happen?

Following this simple and very short rule has often helped me over any hesitancy about asking.

Ask yourself these three questions:

? **1. What is the worst that can happen if I get a 'no'?** (Write these possibilities down.)

? **2. What is the best that can happen if I get a 'yes'?** (Write the potential benefits down.)

? **3. Do the benefits of getting a 'yes' outweigh the downsides of getting a 'no'?**

Once you've run through these questions, I predict that in future you won't hesitate to ask.

Remember, it usually costs nothing to ask!

Think big – ask for the impossible

All too often, the things that we want most appear beyond our reach, so we don't ask for them. The trick is to realize that other people frequently think the same as you. The more attractive something is, the fewer the people there will be who have the personal courage to ask for it.

I have encountered many situations in both my business and personal life where, because something is perceived to be either 'big' or 'important', others have simply failed to ask, leaving the possibility open to me. Be one of the few who ask. You might be surprised and get what you want.

A few years ago I had a client that wanted to raise its national profile in the business world. I suggested that it would be a good idea for them to speak at a particularly high-profile annual business conference. This was not just a minor business event but something that would be attended by thousands of influential people, and covered by national press and the broadcast media. My client laughed at the suggestion, regarding it as ludicrous. This, of course, was just the challenge I needed!

So, I identified who was responsible for the programme of speakers. How did I do that? I rang up and said,

'I wonder if you can help? Who is responsible for organizing your speaking programme for next year's conference, please?' (Hardly brain surgery, is it?)

I then approached the person whose name I had been given. He was actually grateful for my approach, commenting that the bigger the event had got over recent years, the fewer people came forward with an offer to speak.

'People think our platform is out of reach,' he said.

He liked the idea of my client being a speaker. We agreed the topic and, a year later, my client was one of the few lucky ones to climb nervously onto the speaking platform.

Afterwards, an envious competitor of mine, who knew I had arranged this, wanted to know,

'How the hell did you get him up there?'

You know my answer by now:

'I just asked,' I replied.

To give you another simple, personal example:

It was work experience time at my son's school. At a certain age they all have to get themselves a week of work experience. One of the pupils decided to think big. Instead of asking for the possible – a week in a shop or an office – he decided to think big and ask for the impossible. He wrote to 10 Downing Street asking for a job!

Do you know what? He got it!

'A timid question will always receive a confident answer.'

Lord Darling, British Conservative politician and judge (1849–1936)

Ask a cheeky question

Sometimes the more outrageous the question, the more likely you are to get an unexpected 'yes' in reply. Knowing of my fascination with this whole notion of asking cheeky questions, my equally cheeky and fearless teenage son has also taken to asking for things free or at a discount for no other reason than wanting to pay less.

He has often been out with friends to the cinema and, once at the ticket booth, has said to the cashier:

'Can I ask you something? It's going to sound a bit cheeky, but I always believe that if you don't ask you don't get, so how much of a discount are you going to give me?'

Similarly, in shops, when buying something, he has been known to use the same tactic:

'Can I ask you something? It's going to sound a bit cheeky, but I always believe that if you don't ask you don't get, so have you got anything else you can let me have for free?'

Astonishingly, at least 75% of the time he gets a positive result. Although he perhaps doesn't understand why his phrasing of the question is so linguistically powerful, he is clearly doing something right I'll explain exactly what that is later on in the book in the 'Technology of Questions™' section, and explain why it works so well.

Anyway, for now the key message is:

Ask a cheeky question!

Always ask for the price you deserve

Some time ago I took a phone call from an organization that was having what seemed to be an unusual problem.

> 'Can you help us?' they asked. 'We want to reduce the amount of business we are getting.'

> A strange request for someone who usually helps people get more business! Rather curious, I went to see them and they told me,

> 'We are just inundated with work but we don't seem to be making any real money.'

> The real problem was that they were simply too cheap. They were attracting volume business on the back of their low prices. They were afraid to put their prices up and ask existing clients and customers for more on the grounds that they might 'lose their client base,' they told me.

> After a great deal of discussion about the nature of their business, I persuaded them to ask for more and increase their prices by 30%. Having asked for more in the appropriate way, more than 90% of their clients stayed loyal and agreed to pay their higher fees.

The business world is littered with organizations that have consistently underachieved because of their fear of asking for higher prices. As a consequence they have charged at the very lowest level and have attracted high volumes of low-profitability business.

To what extent do you fall into this price trap? Here are a few questions to address:

- ? When was the last time you reviewed your fees and prices?
- ? What do you think would happen if you increased your fees by 10% ... 20% ... 30% or more?
- ? How much of your customer base would you lose if you did?
- ? Would you be better or worse off?

Another key question to ask yourself is:

? What exactly are we selling?

Let me explain. It is just possible that what you perceive you are 'selling' is not the same as what the other party perceives it is buying!

A year or so ago I was chatting with a lawyer about his fees. He told me that for preparing a particular type of document for clients he doesn't like to charge more than £25.

'I would feel guilty charging more than that, as it is a simple form to fill in that only takes me about ten minutes,' he explained.

This seemed very laudable, but when you consider it from a business angle, and that the national average fee for preparing this kind of document is £75, it's clear to see that he was not doing himself any favours.

The lawyer perceived he was selling his time, but the client's perception was that he was getting a document that would give him peace of mind for years to come. Although it might only take the lawyer ten minutes to draft the form, in reality it had taken him years of know-how, experience and judgement to be in a position to recommend this legal device as the solution to the client's problem. This certainly had a greater value to the client than the £25 fee he was charging.

Here's an old joke to remind you of the message here:

A man was driving home one night, in a hurry to get out again to another engagement, when his car broke down. He stopped to open the bonnet in the hope that the problem might be obvious to someone of his limited mechanical know-how. As luck would have it, a car mechanic was passing by on his way home and stopped to offer assistance.

'If I can get it going for you, are you happy to pay a small fee?' asked the mechanic.

'That would be great,' replied the man.

Having looked at the engine for a whole ten seconds, the mechanic said,

'No problem! Close the bonnet and get in the car.'

He then stood over the closed bonnet for a further ten seconds and then banged once gently on it with his hand.

'That should do it,' he proudly announced.

In amazement the man tried the engine and at once it fired into life.

'That's fantastic,' he said. 'How much do I owe you?'

'£25,' came the reply.

'£25 for one little bang on the bonnet!' exclaimed the ungrateful driver.

'No,' replied the mechanic. 'You misunderstand. For the bang on the bonnet I'm only charging you £1. For knowing where to bang I'm charging you the other £24!'

Never forget this. There will be many situations where *you* know where to bang! Always ask for the price that you deserve.

Think about it.

'The wise man questions the wisdom of others because he questions his own, the foolish man, because it is different from his own.'

Leo Stein, US art collector and critic
(1872–1947)

If at first you don't succeed, ask in a different way

What do you do when you ask for something you want and get a 'no' response? I'll tell you what most people do – they give up.

In the introduction to this book, I asked you the following question, and answered it for you:

Do you know what holds you back more than anything else? Well, let me tell you bluntly now. What holds you back is your failure to ASK for what you want...

Now let me add an extra line to this:

... and your failure to ASK for what you want AGAIN if you didn't get the answer you wanted first time around.

That doesn't mean you simply repeat the question over and over and over again like an irritating child. It is more to do with your mindset. Understand and accept that a 'no' in response to a question framed in a particular way at one point in time doesn't mean that it will be a 'no' forever. Remember, things may change. The person you initially got a 'no' from might have since left and the new person might have a different policy, strategy or set of values.

Do not believe the common tip most often given in personal or self-development books – that simply being persistent is the key. You may have heard how Walt Disney's business success was due to him not giving up and asking more than a hundred times for a loan to get him going; how Colonel Sanders's chicken recipe was turned down more than a thousand times and how Sylvester Stallone received a 'no' to his *Rocky* venture over and over again, long before he ever put on a pair of boxing gloves in front of the camera.

Yes, of course persistence is a virtue, and these examples illustrate just that as a strength. However, if you want to get what you want sooner

? 23

rather than later, mere persistence by itself is *not* the answer. What you need to do is to ask yourself two key questions:

? **Why did I get a 'no'?**
? **How can I ask differently?**

As I mentioned, we'll be looking at the many ways you can do this later in the book in the 'Technology of Questions™' section.

Perhaps Walt, The Colonel and Sylvester might have got what they wanted a lot sooner if they had asked in a different way!

'In all affairs it's a healthy thing now and then to hang a question mark on the things you have long taken for granted.'
Bertrand Russell, British author,
mathematician and philosopher
(1872–1970)

Once you have a 'yes', stop asking

Sometimes people assume that getting a 'yes' is going to be so difficult that they keep on talking, asking and persuading long after they have actually succeeded in obtaining a 'yes' response.

What can happen as a result is that they then feed extra information into the situation, which causes the listener to question their initial response.

Once you have had a 'yes', shut up and be pleased!

Don't ask for permission if you're going to do it anyway

Although the entire philosophy of this book is about 'just asking', there are times when you need to have the common sense and discretion to know not to ask at all, and instead to just *do* something. This normally applies to situations where you physically have something within your control or sphere of influence, and which you regard as being so important that you intend to do it anyway. Let me give you a relatively trivial example to illustrate what I'm talking about:

> Some years ago I was chairing a large international business conference in Prague. I was going to be away for four days. Rightly or wrongly, my wife and I thought it would be a valuable and educational experience for my 14-year-old son to come with me to see Prague. So, playing it all by the book, we wrote a formal letter to my son's school summarizing the benefits of his trip to Prague and asking for permission to withdraw him for a few days. Back came a rather formal and no-nonsense note saying, 'We cannot give permission to take your son out of school.'

> Now we had a dilemma. Should we take him anyway and risk the wrath of his school, or should we just let him miss out on this opportunity? I took him anyway. Nothing was said afterwards. What could they do – put me in detention? (Actually there are now restrictions about taking children out of school, so don't do this yourself!)

I have encountered many more serious situations than this, both in my business and personal life, but it taught me a lesson.

Please understand that I am not telling you to ignore authority and disrespect others, but I am suggesting that when faced with these sorts of situations you ask yourself these questions:

? If I ask permission, might they say 'no'?
? Would I do it anyway?

If the answer is 'yes' to both of these, and the consequences of doing it are non-existent, then don't ask at all. Just do it!

Tell the truth, the whole truth and nothing but the truth

Have you ever asked someone for something, but held back from giving them all the details because 'it's none of their business'?

Well, sometimes providing personal details can carry such a tremendous amount of influence that the person you are 'just asking' feels compelled not only to say 'yes', but also to offer even more than you were initially after.

My wife and I recently needed to cancel a holiday because of the illness of one of my sons. In order to cancel the holiday, we needed to notify the hotel, the airline, the car hire company at our planned arrival airport, the car parking at our departure airport and the kennels where we were going to park the dog for a week!

Given that there were less than three weeks to go before the planned holiday, all of the above could legitimately have charged us cancellation fees. I could have simply written or telephoned and said, 'We have to cancel for medical reasons.' After all, the details of my son's illness were hardly the business of the staff at the airline, hotel, car hire, car parking company or even the kennels.

However, I decided this was a time to try out my strategy of asking a question based on the truth, the whole truth and nothing but the truth. So I let them have it. I explained to them,

'It's very disappointing but we have to cancel because, incredibly, my 18-year-old son's lung has just collapsed for a fourth time, despite the fact that he had surgery sometime ago after his third lung collapse to fix it. The hospital has allowed him out of hospital to take his A levels, but after he has the exams out of the way in three weeks' time he will immediately have to have more nasty surgery. Of course he's in pain and discomfort, and the doctors won't allow him to fly. With all that going on, I am ringing to ask you to be generous and understanding over any cancellation costs.'

This level of detail did the job! All were very sympathetic and expressed concern, and some even shared some of their own personal stories. The car park, car hire company and airline all refunded money on the spot. The kennels waived any cancellation costs, and the hotel reduced its cancellation charge from £509 to the £200 deposit.

**Remember, sometimes it pays to ask *and*
give all the details.**

'A sudden bold and unexpected question
doth many times surprise a man and lay
him open.'
*Sir Francis Bacon, English author, courtier
and philosopher (1561–1626)*

Understand the 'some of the time' concept

OK, it's confession time! At some point in this book you'll say to yourself, with me and my asking techniques in mind: 'He must be mad! That's never going to work. I could never say that! Nobody is *ever* going to fall for that.' Well, you know what? You're right.

Throughout the book I've given examples of how I have 'just asked' and, in many cases, got the result that I wanted. Well let me just quell the rumours now. I'm *not* a 'superhero', secretly wearing a brightly-coloured lycra suit emblazoned with a giant question mark on my chest. Sometimes I have failed miserably and tried a different technique or approach, and *still* not got the response that I was after.

Why am I telling you this? Because you need to know that sometimes, whichever technique you use, however you ask, the person or organization you are dealing with will be so stubborn, uncaring, insensitive, bloody-minded, inflexible, uninterested, unpredictable or plain stupid, that the answer you want is not forthcoming.

However, it is sensible to recognize that sometimes the 'gift of yes' is not down to the discretion of the individual you are speaking to, or their company. There may genuinely be valid and understandable reasons why it is simply impossible for them to give you what you want.

My simple message is this: recognize these situations, accept them, don't berate yourself, don't yell at the person you are asking and, above all, don't give up asking again for other things in the future. Essentially, you need to understand that of course the techniques in this book won't work *all* the time but they do work 'some of the time'.

**Your job, having read this book, is
to increase the frequency of
the 'some of the times'.**

Ask for an explanation

How often have you made a decision, gone ahead with a particular course of action or entered into some sort of deal or arrangement without fully understanding the implications?

Do you have a pension? If so, have you got the slightest idea how it all works and whether it really is the best thing to do, or did you just sign and pay? Do you 'pop pills' for some sort of medical problem? If so, do you really know how they are supposed to function, or do you just sip and swallow? Have you ever been asked by a car mechanic, 'Your triple sproddle-woggle has worn down by 3mm to its wingle cog-shaft... Shall we go ahead and replace it?', only to nod your agreement in a daze, wondering what you have just agreed to, and why?

Are you one of the many who admit to falling into these sorts of responses? Why? The usual reasons are being too embarrassed to ask for an explanation because of a subconscious fear of showing ignorance, or concern you won't understand the answer.

The fact is, you might look foolish in the eyes of the person you are dealing with, and indeed you might not understand their answers, especially if they are couched in technical jargon, but so what? What are the consequences? Absolutely none!

You have more to fear from making a decision based on lack of understanding than from being regarded as a fool by the person you are dealing with. So what should you do? Simple – admit to your lack of knowledge and ask for an explanation. If you don't understand, say so, and either ask them to try to explain again in a different way or ask if there is anybody else who might be able to help you understand. Try:

'I'm sorry if I'm a bit slow, but I don't really understand. Would you mind helping me out and explaining it to me in a way that works for me? It's difficult for me to give you an answer or a decision until I am clear on exactly what the issues are.'

You may still struggle, but you should know you can ask and you should try.

Ask for the reaction you want

Have you ever had someone ring you up and ask for your advice, only to object when you give them a response that they didn't want to hear?

'Dad, I'm thinking of doing such and such a thing. What do you think about it?'

'Well, I don't think that's the thing to do right now because...'

Or, have you ever found yourself trying to give practical suggestions to someone who is unloading their terrible day on you, only to be dealt with like you're the enemy and told with some irritation that your moronic 'helpful' offerings are not wanted?

The truth is, people don't necessarily ask for the reaction they want. So, next time you find yourself on the receiving end of the sort of questions mentioned above, try saying to them:

? **Do you mind me asking – is it advice you're after? Or is it really my blessing?**

Or:

? **I'm really sorry you've had such a bad day. Do you mind me asking, are you looking for possible solutions? Or are you just wanting to get things off your chest?**

Once you know what the person is really after, it's much easier to couch your response in a way that is going to be most constructive. Similarly, if it is *you* who is after a particular reaction, be precise about what you are after.

If you want someone's blessing, a shoulder to cry on, approval, praise, practical advice, creative suggestions, a hug, personal criticism, directions, an apology, more attention, a date, a meeting, a favour, a loan, help, a lift, a discount, more time… then 'just ask'.

Be precise at the outset and state exactly what it is you are after. Don't ever get frustrated about a person's inability to read your mind!

Build rapport

A person is much more likely to agree to a favour if they like you. If you are getting on with someone they will find it harder to turn you down. So if you know you are going to want to ask them for something, and there is a real possibility they might say 'no', go out of your way to be extra helpful and friendly.

I recently had a telephone engineer in my home doing some engineering work. It had taken four phone calls over a three-week period, some of which had lasted 40 minutes, to navigate my way through the maze of infuriating organizational 'red tape' just to get them to understand what I wanted and the job booked in.

Only on the day of the job itself did I remember that we actually needed something else doing to our phone that was totally unrelated to the purpose of the visit. Call me a cynic, but long experience of dealing with this organization told me that if I asked them officially, it would involve another four phone calls, and that I would be charged again for someone coming out to my home. Rather pointless, I thought, when I already had someone about to arrive.

Now, despite what you think, I am not usually manipulative, and by nature I'm pretty easy-going and friendly. On this occasion, however, I decided I would ask the engineer to do the additional job for me as a personal favour.

Firstly, I wanted to get him in a state where it would be hard to say 'no'. So, as soon as he arrived he was greeted with,

'I've just put the kettle on. Tea or coffee?'

He was offered chocolate biscuits and, whilst we drank and ate together, I made conversation with him.

'So how long have you been doing this sort of work? How did you get into it? So what sort of changes over the years have you seen?'

He became very chatty and we had a nice warm and friendly conversation about his 'life and works', his family holiday to Greece, and even about some of his future plans.

By the time I got around to asking him whether he would mind doing me a personal favour and sort out this other problem for me, there was only one possible answer he could give...

'No problem! Let me take a look at it for you.'

The rule is simple:

**If you want to ask someone a favour,
try to build rapport with them first!**

'Computers are useless. They can only
give you answers.'
*Pablo Picasso, Spanish cubist painter
(1881–1973)*

Narrow down your questions

Sometimes you will be asked questions, in your business or personal life, that are so general you'll find them almost impossible to answer. A favourite in personal development books or seminars is, *'What are your goals?'* Have you ever been asked this? Have you ever felt frustrated and inadequate because you don't have an instant answer, or because the replies that do spring to mind seem woolly and superficial?

If you are in business, at some point in your career some clever so-and-so will ask you, with your business in mind, 'What is your strategic plan for where you want the business to be in five years' time?'

Do you find yourself starting to sweat as you drift effortlessly into vague, meaningless 'executive speak' in reply? You hope your answer sounds convincing, but you know deep down that it could be roughly translated as, 'What the hell are you talking about? I haven't the faintest idea!'

It *is* OK to feel frustrated by questions such as these because, although they are important issues to address, they are incredibly poorly framed, and almost impossible to answer effectively. The reason for this is that they are simply too wide. The lesson here is, if you want to get a proper answer from someone, narrow down your question and focus on something specific to which there *is* an answer.

Rather than a general question about your 'goals', imagine if you had been asked, for example, more specific questions, such as:

? Do you plan to have children? How many do you think you would like?
? Do you plan to get married?
? Do you see yourself living in this country or abroad?
? What sort of house would you ideally like to live in?
? Are you looking to stay in this job permanently?

Isn't it the case that, if you were asked narrow questions like these, you would be able to focus on and answer each one in turn, ultimately forming a clearer picture of your 'goals roadmap'?

Let me give you another simple example, this time on a much more domestic and straightforward level. Imagine someone's birthday is coming up and, instead of just surprising them, you decide to ask them what they would like. Have you ever asked, 'Any ideas what I can get you for your birthday?', only to be greeted with an embarrassed, 'Well... I don't know. Nothing really springs to mind.'?

Again, the problem is that the question is too broad. Suppose you narrowed it down:

? If someone were to buy you a CD, which one would you like?

? If you were in a book shop with a voucher, what book would you choose?

I'll guarantee you'll get a specific answer.

Let me repeat the rule:

**Narrow down your question and
you'll get a more productive answer.**

'It is error only, and not truth, that shrinks from inquiry.'

*Thomas Paine, US patriot and political
philosopher (1737–1809)*

How does the other party benefit?

A client of mine recently proudly told me how their company had been marketing a specific service of their business. They told me about the letter which they had optimistically sent out to 700 organizations in a particular field asking for referrals. I was impressed – after all, as you know by now, I very much encourage people to ask for what they want. The problem was, however, as they went on to tell me, that they had not yet received a single response or referral.

'So much for asking,' one of the partners complained. 'It doesn't work!'

I responded with a question:

'What benefits do the people you wrote to get by sending you business?'

There was an embarrassed silence in the room, as the three partners stared at each other. Eventually, one of them sheepishly looking down said,

'Well there aren't any, really.'

The point was already made. I hardly needed to say it, but I did.

'Well, that's why you haven't had anything back from your letter.'

The point here is really very simple. Although I have told you in several places in the book already not to hesitate to ask for what you want, on the basis that 'some of the time' you'll get it, it does, however, pay to first ask yourself:

? **What is the benefit to the other person in giving me what I want?**

In business, of course, there are a number of obvious possible benefits for the other party, such as:

- money;
- business introductions;
- goods or services as a swap;
- information.

Consider these options. If you aren't sure which of them, if any, is going to do the trick, then ask them point-blank. For example:

? Is there anything we can do for you that might prompt you to consider sending us referrals?

On a personal level the same applies. If there isn't any obvious benefit for the other person, try to think of something before you ask. Believe it or not, however, sometimes all you have to offer in return for a personal favour is your genuine gratitude. People like to be valued, and we all get a warm feeling from simply doing a good deed for someone else.

With this in mind, always preface your question with something that indicates you are really going to appreciate the gesture. You could try:

? How would you like to be a lifesaver?

? If you could do me a small favour I'd be hugely grateful.

? I know it's a lot to ask, but...

Next time you are going to ask for something, then, remember:

Always ask yourself first, how does the other person benefit?

Say what you mean – don't hold back

Now here's a curious thing! Every couple of months or so the salesperson for a particular company pushes an expensive, glossy catalogue of their products through the door with an order form paper-clipped to it. Two days later he rings the doorbell, like a child asking for his ball back, and without fail the question he asks is,

'I've come to collect the catalogue. Can I have it back please?'

I hand it over and he goes on his way, only to return a few weeks later to repeat the process.

I'm beginning to feel sorry for him. (Perhaps that's the real strategy!) As far as he's concerned, the purpose of his second visit is to collect orders, and I suspect that, in his mind, when he asks for the magazine back, he thinks he is doing exactly that.

What he ought to be doing is asking me something like:

? Have you had enough time to look through the catalogue? Or do you need more time to decide what you want to order this time?

? I'm from the catalogue company. I left you the magazine the other day. Can I have your completed order form please?

? Have you seen the special offer on the 'coffee-making-towel-rack' on page 37?

The overall message is very simple:

Say what you mean. Don't hold back!
Ask for *precisely* what you want.

Adopt the 'How can I...?' mindset

The word '**how**' is extremely important in this book. There's a lot I want to say about it. Once you understand its power, it has the potential to be one of your most valuable 'just asking' tools.

So important is it, that each time I sat down to write, I was beating myself up over the question of where to put it: should I put it in with the Golden Rules? Does it belong in the 'Technology of Questions™' section or should it go in Questions To 'Just Ask' Yourself?

I've finally come up with the obvious answer! I don't have to be limited by my own question, and so I have decided to include it in *each* section. So the 'how' issue will make several guest appearances in this book, each time from a slightly different standpoint

First of all I want you to think of the word 'how' as a rule of 'just asking'.

How often have you heard people say 'I can't'? How many times have you said it yourself, whether out loud, or to yourself? In your life there are likely to have been numerous examples of times when you (or others) have given this response in reply to a key question. But this simple little phrase is one of the most self-limiting expressions in existence!

Let's look at a few possible examples, in a personal, business and professional context:

'How about doing a seriously long fundraising walk or run?'

'I can't. I'm not fit enough.'

'If you don't like that job, why don't you stop doing it and change to something else?'

'I can't. I'm stuck where I am. I have too many expenses to risk a change.'

'Why don't you call company X? I'm sure they'd be interested in your goods or services.'

'I can't get past the managing director's gatekeeper!'

'Why don't you ask him out?'

'I can't. I don't know him!'

Before we go any further, it's important to distinguish **'I can't'** from various other simple, and possibly perfectly valid, excuses such as:

'I don't want to.'

'I'm afraid to make a change.'

'I've tried before without any success.'

'I'm scared of rejection.'

If, however, you *would* like to make these things happen, all you have to do is adopt the 'how' mindset. This simply means exchanging your *'I can't'* response for the question,

? 'How can I do that?'

Going back to the first example, if someone suggested doing a fundraising walk or run to you, and you were interested in the idea, instead of replying with, **'I can't** – I'm not fit enough,' stop and ask the question,

? 'How can I get fit enough?'

Focus on answers to that question, and then act upon them.

Similarly, if you are tempted to make a career change in your life, instead of simply saying **'I can't'** again, change tack and think in terms of the question,

? 'How? How can I do that?'

In fact, ask yourself that question whenever you hear yourself saying **'I can't'**. The moment you do so, two things happen. First, there is a part of your unconscious mind that actually accepts the possibility that perhaps you 'can', and second, it changes your focus. This approach will get you thinking of options and methods to overcome whatever obstacles you claimed were holding you back.

What's the most obvious solution?

Sometimes the answer to a problem or issue is so obvious that we miss it. With this in mind, when you are struggling to know what to do, where to find something or how to make something happen, it can be astonishingly successful to actually ask yourself:

? **What's the most obvious solution?**

When you have an answer, consider following it regardless of how bizarre it seems! Let me give you a personal example.

> 6.30 p.m.: a calm evening in the Cooper household. All of a sudden there was a loud and excited yell from the lounge.
>
> 'Come quickly! She's on television!' shouted my son, who was glued to the screen.
>
> My wife and I dashed into the room and there was my daughter on the screen! This wasn't actually all that surprising – she is an actress after all. But the item we were watching turned out to be a short clip from a new feature film, which was being premiered at a major Leeds cinema that night at a glittering champagne opening. Yorkshire Television was covering the item on its local news programme, and was interviewing the film's director.
>
> Not only had we not known about this event, neither had my daughter, who had played a small role in the film. Nevertheless, as it was local, we wanted to be part of it. So what could we do? My wife grabbed the local paper to see what time the premiere began, and my son hit the internet. But, although both gave the times for showings of the film later that week, neither mentioned the time of the premiere. My wife rang the cinema box office, which told us the same.
>
> 6.40 p.m.: 'Time for the magic question,' I thought. So I went somewhere quiet and asked myself, 'We want to be part of this event. What is the most obvious way of making it happen?' The answer I came up with was to contact the director himself and ask if we could attend the premiere. But how would I do that? Again the

? 41

answer was obvious: ring the television channel where he had just appeared and ask to speak to him. So this is what I did. *(Note the number of questions along the way.)* I got the number of Yorkshire Television from the phonebook and rang them.

'Good evening. Yorkshire Television. How may I help you?'
'Could you put me through to the green room for the programme that's going out please?'

I was put through to the production team on the programme.

'I've just watched your interview with the director of film X. My daughter's one of the actresses in the film. Is the director still in the green room?' I asked.

'No, he's just left to go to the premiere. It starts in 30 minutes,' I was told.

'Oh dear! I wonder, how can you help me contact him then?' I asked. (Note the use of the words 'how' and 'help'.)

'Well, I shouldn't, but I suppose I could give you his mobile number,' came the very helpful and rather surprising reply.

6.50 p.m.: I dialled the mobile number and found myself speaking to the director's wife, who answered the phone. I explained the situation and politely asked for three tickets to the premiere. After a couple of minutes' silence while she checked, she returned to the phone and said,

'There will be three complimentary tickets waiting for you at our reception. We look forward to seeing you later.'

7.00 p.m.: We jumped into the car for a mad dash to the cinema and, by 7.20 p.m., took our seats just as the director was greeting the media, main stars of the film and his guests! Three hours later, filled with both champagne and parental pride, we returned home clutching our film premiere 'goody bags', and reflected on the evening.

Apart from the fact that it was all most enjoyable, the real moral of this story is that you should ask yourself the question, 'What is the obvious solution?' and then act on it!

If you want a different answer, ask a different person

If you don't like the answer you have been given, it's OK to ask someone else. There have been countless times when I have done just that, with great results, almost without realizing what I was doing. It has worked both in major business transactions and with minor, domestic personal issues.

If I want to make something happen in my business or personal life, and my approach or question is turned down, my first conscious thought is not to give up but to ask myself:

> **?** Who else in that organization can I ask, who might give me the answer I want?

I have learned from experience that there are many reasons why a second person might give me a different answer from the first, which is why I now know that it's worth asking. The first person, for instance, might have been in a bad mood, depressed, stressed, not well, have just had a row with their partner, mother-in-law or boss, have been tired, fed up with the job, running late for a meeting, trying to do today's sudoku 'killer' puzzle or simply attempting to watch the football on a portable television they had smuggled into the office!

They may simply not like you, not have the authority to give you the answer you want, not understand what you're asking for (nor see the benefits to them), or they may just be plain 'bloody-minded jobsworths' who enjoy saying 'no'. At its simplest, you may be dealing with someone in a call or customer services centre pushing buttons on a computer, who has, quite literally, pressed the wrong buttons.

Conversely, the 'someone else' you ask might have a different opinion on the matter, be in a great mood, be keen to be helpful and service-driven, and actually enjoy being able to give a 'yes' response. Again, if an administrative process is involved, they may simply look at different things on their computer screen.

Let's look at a few simple examples. In my business life I have made many approaches over the years, to hundreds of organizations, trying to pitch various services or ideas for myself or clients, only to be very bluntly turned down. When this has happened, I have, on many occasions, simply picked up the phone again, spoken to a different person in the organization and got a different answer.

I know what you're thinking! Isn't the first person likely to get annoyed and possibly offended that you have asked one of their colleagues, or gone over their head? Well, sometimes yes, and sometimes no. If they do get annoyed or offended, then you need to ask yourself, 'Well, so what?' Is it better to have to deal with the occasional potential political hassle in the most diplomatic way possible, or to give up the benefits of getting the answer you want for a quiet life? It's your decision.

On a more mundane, personal level, I have often called restaurants, hotels, train or plane reservation centres to make a booking only to be told they were fully booked. Whenever this happens, I either instantly call back, or wait until I can be reasonably sure I won't get the same person. I ask the same question and at least half the time I get a different response.

I have also, over the years, often made calls asking for the price of things. If I don't like the figure I am given I call back another time, and speak to someone else. Without any argument or pressing, again in at least 50% of cases, I am given a different, and better, price.

> My wife was ringing around recently for a car insurance quote, and was given a figure of £916. I suggested she put this particular Golden Rule to the test and call them back to try again. Rather cynically she agreed. This time a different person at the same call centre quoted her £611 for the same insurance cover.
>
> Asking a different person saved us £305!

Prepare to be asked

Have you ever been in a job interview and been floored by a question? How often have you been in a business meeting and been asked something that you weren't prepared for, then found yourself waffling with as much professional confidence as you could muster? The fact is, there will be times in your life when you are not doing the asking, but are on the receiving end of a grilling from someone else.

There is a simple, common-sense trick to minimize the risks and stresses of these sorts of situations, which again involves 'just asking'. This time, however, the question needs to be directed at yourself. So, before entering certain situations, ask yourself:

? **What questions am I likely to be asked, and how can I best answer them?**

Make a list of them.

If you are going for a job interview, whilst you can't be absolutely certain what you will be asked, you can make a list based on obvious possibilities. If you are in a business sales situation, there are some obvious questions you are likely to get about your particular goods or services. List these questions, and plan how you would deal with them in advance.

I'll share with you how I learnt this very simple trick, which some of you might find useful if you ever have to deal with the media.

Some years ago I was being interviewed on various radio and television programmes about one of my early books. I would very nervously put the headphones on in the radio studio or climb on to the cosy couch for a breakfast television programme, worried about the questions I would have to face and the millions of people who were potentially going to think I was an idiot.

Then I realized, after the first few experiences, that almost all the questions I was being asked were along the same lines. With this thought in mind I decided to prepare myself by pretending I was the interviewer and writing a list of all the questions I could think of that I might ask 'me'. I then worked out in advance all the possible answers to those questions, and even practised them at home.

Using this method, not only did I give better performances on the programmes, but I was also less stressed.

So next time you enter question situations yourself, remember this Golden Rule:

Prepare to be asked!

'If you do not ask the right questions, you do not get the right answers. A question asked in the right way often points to its own answer. Asking questions is the A-B-C of diagnosis. Only the inquiring mind solves problems.'

Edward Hodnett, US poet (1841–1920)

Ask someone who knows the answers

Some people seem to be temperamentally averse to asking questions. If the most basic purpose of asking is simply to get information, why is it that so many of us go out of our way to avoid this terrifying ordeal? I'll give you a few examples:

> I have a close relative who simply refuses to ask directions to places when he is driving in unfamiliar territory. He has even been known to overtake me when following in his car, when I knew the way and he didn't.

> Then there are those clients who won't ask me for help or comments on the presentations they have to give because, as they are quick to point out, 'You might tell us what's wrong with what we're going to do.'

> And finally, we have friends who have stayed in hotels in our city without asking us first which ones were most decent or convenient, and which to avoid.

The point is this. There will be hundreds of situations in all aspects of your life where you will have to do things, go to places or make decisions based on what *you* know. But by asking others who have faced these things before, who have more experience or greater knowledge than you, you increase your chances of getting things right.

Always ask yourself:

? **Who knows the answers, or has the experience?**

Ask questions 'outside the box'

You've heard of 'thinking outside the box'. What I would like you to do now is think about *'asking questions* outside the box'. The questions you come up with might seem radical and downright stupid, but the mental exercise can prove extremely interesting, sometimes fruitful and, failing that, at least fun!

My oldest son, a real creative thinker, came up with this little gem:

'Dad, I've checked it out. If it costs £25 to change your name by deed poll and thousands of pounds to buy a personalized car number plate, why don't people just change their name to match the number plate they already have?'

Of course, this is a bizarre and impractical notion, and I am not suggesting you should do it, but isn't it a great question? It's a classic example of challenging traditional thoughts and ideas. The fact is, sometimes we do things and take certain decisions in life simply because it is the expected and normal thing to do. I have learned through many of my own experiences, and from those of other people, that sometimes standing back and challenging the norm can pay real dividends.

A close friend recently confided in me with a tale about his ageing mother.

Some years ago my mother decided to put her property up for sale as she wanted to buy a small flat for £50,000 in sheltered and managed accommodation. At that time her house went on the market for £60,000. Mother stressed for months about whether she was going to get a buyer in time to secure the flat she wanted. Luckily, she did sell it and was able to move into her chosen flat.

Looking back, however, had we asked ourselves a different question at the time and not allowed her to just get sucked into selling first in order to fund the purchase, as everyone else does, she might have gone down a different route. We didn't think of it at the time, but the truth was she could have immediately bought her new flat out of her life's savings and moved without first selling her existing property.

She could then have kept the first property and let it out to bring in rental income to live off. This would have left her better off, with the income massively exceeding the bank interest and she would still own the first property, which is now worth £240,000!

I must stress that I am not trying to pass on property advice – I have limited knowledge of this area. The moral of the story, however, is very interesting in the context of this book and certainly deserves a place in my Golden Rules of asking questions.

There will be times when you should ask yourself the question:

? **I know this is what most people do in these sort of situations, but is it the best way forward or is there a different approach?**

The mere act of asking this question may trigger a different thought pattern, and ultimately better results.

> 'No man really becomes a fool until he stops asking questions.'
> *Charles P. Steinmetz, US mathematician and electrical engineer (1865–1923)*

If someone asks you for help, put yourself out

Some people are naturally helpful and like to say 'yes'. Others, however, have lost sight of what it's like to need help. If you are successful and busy in your job or personal life, how willing are *you* to give others your time, advice, contacts and to create opportunities for them when you're asked to do so?

> When I was 18, I was interested in a possible career in television journalism. Even then I must have realized the potential benefits of asking because, either being naive or a bit cheeky, I wrote to the late, much-missed broadcaster, Richard Whitely, who at that time was one of two broadcast journalists who hosted Yorkshire Television's 'Calendar' news programme.
>
> I told him I was interested in what he did and asked him if he would mind giving me some time for some advice and guidance. I got a personal letter back from Richard inviting me to spend an afternoon with him as he prepared for the programme. He took me behind the scenes, was very generous with his time, offered advice and gave me an insight into a world I had not experienced before. Many years later I met him once more at a social event, thanked him again, and reminded him of this gesture. He answered with a smile,
>
> 'I always like to say "yes" to people on their way up. After all, you never know when you might meet them again – when you are on your way down!'

Be gentle – ask questions sensitively

Questions aren't simply a way of obtaining information, or getting something you want. They also have the power to change the way people feel. Questions influence what people focus on, and their mood, so be careful what you ask!

At its simplest, asking a positive question will make someone search for a positive response and, more often than not, they will attach good feelings to the experience. Ask them a negative question, however, and you force the brain to search for negatives. These have the potential to adversely affect how someone feels. A simple example for you:

> My wife and I were at a social event recently and met some people who had been brought up in London, but who had moved to Birmingham for work reasons. Making small talk, my wife asked a positive question:

> 'So how do you like Birmingham?'

> The question encouraged a positive focus and response, and the person extolled the virtues of living in Birmingham with a smile on her face. They chatted for a while. My wife then said:

> 'Let me ask you a different question. What do you miss most about London?'

> There was a pause, the mood dropped, and you could almost physically see the lady on the receiving end process this negative question in a different way. Her facial expressions changed as we heard her talk sadly about the friends they missed and the family members they couldn't see as often.

Here are a few more mood-changing questions you might have either asked, or have been asked. Take a look at them and decide for yourself whether they are positive or negative. Each of them compels you to search for a certain kind of response – a response that will affect how you feel:

? **So what else can go wrong today?**
? **How's your pain level?**

?   How do you manage to keep coming up with all those ideas?
?   So, how are you coping with all that stress?
?   How many more are you going to sell today?
?   So you're going on holiday to X? Aren't you worried about the
    recent terrorist attacks there?
?   Oh, you've booked with Coach Company Y. Did you know that they
    have the worst safety record of all coach companies?
?   So X is doing your operation? Did you know he's one of the top
    surgeons for that type of problem?

The basic rule is this:

Be kind; ask yourself first how this question is going to make someone feel. If it's going to make someone feel good, ask it. If not, don't bother, unless you deliberately want to force someone to focus on the negatives.

'It is not the answer that enlightens, but
the question.'
Eugène Ionesco, French (Romanian-born)
absurdist dramatist (1909–1994)

THE 'TECHNOLOGY OF QUESTIONS™'

So far, we've looked at what I've called the **Golden Rules of 'Just Asking'**. By now you have probably recognized yourself in at least some of the issues I've raised – maybe you've even fallen into some of the traps I've described? You might even have said to yourself, 'That's basic stuff! I know that!' If that's the case, then good, but why then have you continually ignored the simplicity of what you already know?

It's now time to take a look at what I call the **'Technology of Questions™'** and examine some of the easiest, and most effective, techniques for asking for whatever it is you want.

The power of influence

There is a great danger of me getting too scientific in this section. I could spend the next hundred pages pretending to write an academic and theoretical textbook, encapsulating advanced linguistic patterns and explaining the paradoxical and habitual expectations of the unconscious mind, and its relationship with the philosophy of quantum primary negative language injunctions... Or I could just keep it simple, short and practical! Which would you prefer?

Let me be even more blunt. You don't need to understand *why* these techniques work. The purpose of this book is not to make you smarter, but more successful. There is, however, just one overriding principle you *do* need to understand. I'll sum it up in one word:

Influence!

You need to know that each technique is not geared simply towards *you* and what *you* want, but on what to say, how to say it, or how to behave, so that it *influences* the other person to give the response you're after. Essentially, you are about to become an 'influence guru'! With this in mind, the only bit of theory you need to know is that:

Questions exert a greater level of influence than anything else. Ask someone a question and it forces them to focus on that issue.

Wherever possible, don't *tell*, but *ask*. *Tell* somebody something and the mind will accept, ignore or not even hear it. *Ask* them about the same thing, and their brain is literally compelled to process the question and search for an answer – and the answer they come up with will influence them to feel, behave or respond in a specific way.

Let me tell you about a simple experiment I did at a recent live seminar of mine to prove the point:

> I noticed as I arrived at the venue that the air conditioning unit had a gentle background hum. As I began my morning seminar I told the delegates in a very matter-of-fact way,
>
> 'Sorry about the bit of noise from the air conditioning unit. Now, today we are going to talk about...',

and I launched straight into my material. Nobody took a blind bit of notice of the gentle hum of the noise I had mentioned.

Later that day, in the afternoon session, with a different group of delegates, I didn't mention or tell them about the noise at all until about half-way through. This time, however, I asked them a question about it. I paused and then said,

'I'm sorry to hold things up, but is the noise from the air conditioning unit distracting anyone?'

I paused again. Around the room people started to process the question. They listened. All of a sudden there was a deathly silence and, sure enough, all you could hear was the hum of the air conditioning unit!

I had complaints afterwards that asking this had put people off.

'I hadn't heard the damn thing till you asked that question. Once you had asked it I couldn't hear anything else!' commented one delegate.

I got the same response from several others.

Wicked person that I was, by raising the issue as a question I had brought the hum to everyone's attention and made them realize just how annoying it was. Whilst it irritated some of my delegates, the experiment did show how much power and influence a question can have, as opposed to simply telling people things.

By the way, where are you reading this book? If you're in bed, is the 'tick-tock' from the clock bothering you? If you are at home during the day, is the traffic noise from outside a distraction?

See what I mean? Sorry!

Ask the right person

If you want to get the answer you want, your first task is to consciously ask yourself:

? **Who is the best person to ask?**

Remember, this might not be the most senior person in an organization. Always choose the person who is most likely to give you the response you want. Take your time and think about it first. Identify the right person and, if necessary, *wait* until you can see or speak to them. Don't be tempted to ask someone else. If you ask the wrong person, don't be surprised if you get the wrong answer.

Sometimes, of course, you may not know who the right person is. So what do you do? Ask! Don't assume – find out! If necessary, contact the organization or whoever can guide you on this and ask:

? **I wonder if you can help me. I need to know who to talk to about...**

? **Sorry to disturb, but would you mind telling me who is the person responsible for...?**

Ask at the right time

However great you are at actually asking for what you want, there is another very important, simple technique you must learn, and that's **timing**. If there's someone you want to approach with a question, you actually need to ask yourself:

? When's the best time to do the asking?

The simple answer is that the best time is whenever that person is going to be most likely to give you the answer you want, or at least be in the most receptive state to hear and focus on your request. Let me give you a few examples.

It might be that you want to ask your boss for a salary increase, or about your future prospects. In this sort of situation, you want to be sure you catch him or her at a time when they can give you their undivided attention. You wouldn't want to be asking these questions when it is obvious your boss is under pressure to get an important document out, in the middle of resolving some irritating crisis, or when they are expecting an important phone call.

So, be patient. Think – when is the best time?

Of course, you could take control and set things up for yourself by asking your boss that very question:

? I know how busy you are at the moment, but I need a few minutes with you privately to discuss something important. When is good for you?

Every business needs to know that sales is an area where the timing of key questions is of paramount importance. Often the difference between getting the sale and not getting it is simply down to asking for the business either too early or late.

My daughter bought my wife and me a surprise half-hour photography session. It was done at a special rate as a promotional gimmick for the photographer, in order to get people into his studio. We knew that, and good luck to him for his initiative! It worked on the basis that he gave customers on this deal a 'free picture', regardless of whether they decided to go ahead and order anything else or not. It seemed like a 'win-win' situation for all concerned.

So we arrived at the photographer's – my wife and I and our three grown-up offspring – all with combed hair, clean teeth and wearing the colour-coordinated clothes my daughter insisted we wear!

Within seconds of walking through his studio door, long before we had posed for any pictures, let alone seen them, the photographer asked us,

'What would you like to buy in addition to the "free" one you've already paid for? Would you like the 9 x 7 at £550? A framed 10 x 8 for £1,250, or a circular picture on a 15 x 12 canvas at £1,750? It's better if I ask you now,' he said, 'so I don't have to waste too much time on you if you just want the "free" one.'

So what do you think of his timing, and how do you think this made us feel?

For the benefit of any reader who has to 'sell' things, and that is everybody, *never* try to close the sale by asking for the business until after you have established a real 'want' in the customer. In this example, the photographer shouldn't even have raised the 'further purchase' issue until we were sitting down viewing the photos he had taken, and cooing lustfully over them.

(Oh, and by the way, we decided just to have the 'free' photo my daughter had paid for! Well, we would have done if the photographer hadn't 'accidentally' deleted it!)

Out of interest, it's worth noting that, without wishing to appear manipulative, there are also times when it can be positively beneficial to ask your question when people *are* busy and under pressure. Sometimes you can get the quick, snap answer you want if you frame it well, because the person doesn't have the time to debate things with you.

Of course, this technique of choosing the right time to ask is extremely important in your personal life too. For example, don't ask someone for a personal favour at the most inopportune moment.

Someone I know well rang recently whilst I was having dinner with my family. They wanted to ask me something:

'Look I'm just eating, I'll call you back,' I told them.

'It won't take long – I just wanted to ask you...,' they replied, launching into their request.

My response? Well, had they been patient enough to hold back on their request, they may have got closer to their desired answer.

As far as relationships are concerned, this principle is everything. Romantics will know that choosing the right moment to ask someone out on a date, or to marry them, is key to getting the magic 'yes'.

If you want to be sure of the answer you want, then pIck the right moment to ask!

'If you want a wise answer, ask a reasonable question.'

Johann Wolfgang Von Goethe, German dramatist, novelist, poet and scientist (1749–1832)

Ask in the right environment

Picture this. We've all seen films where soft music is playing in the background and the sound of waves can be heard lapping on to the sandy beach. The sun is setting over a vista of palm trees, and the romantic male lead goes down on one knee and asks the female lead to marry him. With glistening eyes she says, 'Yes.' The music gets louder, the question has been asked satisfactorily ... job done!

I know this all sounds a bit over-sentimental and predictable, but actually there is a simple lesson to be learnt from this example. The environment in which you do the asking can play a part in maximizing the chances of getting the response you want to a question you're planning to ask.

Of course you won't always have the chance to control the place where you're going to do the asking but, if you do, at the very least take it into account. Ask yourself the question:

? **Is there any place, situation or environment where it will be either easier to ask my question, or harder for the person to say 'no'?**

If there is, do what you can to organize this.

If you're in business, then the sort of questions you might ask yourself, if you want to raise an issue with a customer, client, prospect or other contact, are:

? **Should we meet in my office or theirs?**
? **Should we meet over a desk in a formal setting, or over lunch?**
? **Should it be somewhere quiet or very lively?**
? **Should I take a colleague with me? If so, who?**
? **Should I wait until a large business networking function?**
? **Should I take them on some impressive corporate hospitality event?**
? **Should I save my question for the golf course?**
? **Should I do the asking in the changing room at the gym?**
? **Am I better chatting over a quick pint in the pub at lunchtime?**

I can't give you a definite answer because each of these will be right at some time or other, depending on the situation, what it is you want to ask and, of course, the personalities involved. The important thing is to understand that you shouldn't just ignore the issue and leave it to pure chance.

Always ask yourself: where is the best place to do the asking?

'You can tell whether a man is clever by his answers. You can tell whether a man is wise by his questions.'

Naguib Mahfouz,
Egyptian novelist (1911–2006)

? 63

Who should do the asking?

If there's something you want, you don't always have to ask for it yourself. It's an important and perfectly valid strategy and technique to consider the possibility that someone else could 'just ask' for you.

So, ask yourself early on:

? **Am I the best person to do the asking?**

Or

? **Who might be better than me at getting the desired outcome?**

There are two reasons why it might be appropriate or advisable to get someone else to do the asking for you. First, they may simply be better at it than you. Don't underestimate this point. In my business dealings I see it illustrated on an almost daily basis, with organizations getting the wrong people to represent them in 'sales' or 'asking' situations.

Whilst everyone is capable of improving their questioning skills, it is a fact that some people are simply better at it than others. If, indeed, you have access to someone who is consistently better than you at getting what they want and making things happen, and they are willing to do the asking for you, then it makes sense to get their support.

It might simply be that the person you're hoping will do the asking for you has an existing relationship with the person on the receiving end of the question. If this is the case, your chances of success are immediately increased.

Alternatively, it may not be a question of ability, but one of influence and 'leverage'. Maybe, because of a person's reputation or their position within an organization, their question will be perceived as carrying greater weight and therefore be harder to turn down.

I was consulted by an organization last year that wanted my help. They wanted to target a certain company for business, and I was asked how best they should make the approach. One of the early issues I got them to think about was not just 'how' the approach should be made but 'who' should make it? In spite of my protestations, initially all fingers were pointing at me, until I asked them whether anyone in the organization had ever dealt with anyone at the target company before. 'Yes,' said one of my client's senior people. 'I went to school with their finance director, and I see him once a week to play squash!'

Unless my client was simply too embarrassed to make the initial approach himself, it's fairly obvious that his request would be likely to carry a greater level of leverage and influence than mine. My client would be contacting someone he knows well, whilst I would be calling up totally cold, fighting my way past the gatekeeper in the hope that I might be able to influence a total stranger. I could, of course, have used the name of my client to get past the gatekeeper: 'So-and-so asked me to call.' But my client's friend is going to think it very strange that his own ex-school and squash-playing pal didn't have the bottle to ask himself.

> Having persuaded my client to make the initial approach for the reasons just given, I then prompted him to ask the finance director who in his organization had the gift of work, and could make the decision about using my client in the future. Most importantly, I got my client to ask his friend,

> 'Would you mind doing me a favour and speaking to your colleague about us, giving us an introduction, and maybe seeing if he will meet us?'

Because the question came from the finance director to another internal senior colleague, the level of leverage was considerable. The result was that my client was in through the door and, some months later, after a series of meetings, some business was secured.

Of course, there are personal situations where this technique is important too:

> One of my daughter's friends approached me as she knew I had various contacts in the media at that time. She asked me if I would be willing to ask one of my contacts if he would give her a week of work experience in his media organization. I did and he immediately agreed.

So, before jumping in with your questions, ask yourself first:

Who should do the asking?

Ask someone what *they* would do

Have you ever been in a situation where you have asked a question but you can't get a straight answer out of someone? Maybe you've asked a professional for advice? Just recently, a consultant I was seeing for a medical problem mentioned three places I could go for physiotherapy.

'It's up to you which you choose. They can all help you,' he told me.

Here is a simple question technique, which gets you the answer you want more often than not. I have used it many times with great success.

Ask the person what *they* would do.

Here is what I asked my consultant in response to his comment about choosing a physiotherapist:

'OK,' I said. 'Well let me ask you this, then. If it were you or a member of your family who needed treatment, which one of the three physiotherapists you have just mentioned would you go to?' Without a moment's hesitation he answered.

'Oh, I'd go to Sarah.' And he gave me the name and address of a specific person. 'She's very good,' he added with a knowing nod.

Job done! This is an easy and very effective technique to learn.

Change a negative into a positive

Have you ever asked for something and been told in reply, 'No, we/you can't do that.'? In business you might have heard:

'No, we can't get the delivery to you by then – we're rushed off our feet at the moment.'

'No, that's our lowest price. We can't go any lower.'

'The computer system won't allow that, so we can't do it.'

Maybe, on a personal or social level, you have been told by a restaurant you want to go to, for example:

'No, we're full. We can't fit you in.'

'No, you can't hold your meetings there because of the noise factor.'

You could always give in to these various responses, *or* you could try one of my two special question techniques, both of which have the power to change the focus of the person who is giving you a negative response and encourage them to look for positives.

When you hear 'I can't...' try asking a question that begins with:

?   If you *were* able to...

Or

?   How *can* we/you...

Let me give you some examples of both. You can then choose and adapt either to suit your purpose. These are real examples where I have been able to use them successfully.

The 'If you *were* able to...' technique

There's one particular restaurant where we like to eat every now and then on a Sunday. I rang them up and asked for a table, to be told,

'Sorry, we're full! We're really busy that day, and we just can't fit you in.' You should know by now that a response like that merely

? 67

sets me a challenge. So, I tried one of my own Golden Rules. I rang back, spoke to someone else, and asked the same question. On this occasion I got the same answer: 'Sorry, we're really busy that day. We can't fit you in.' OK, I thought. What else? I decided to unleash the 'If you *were* able to...' technique. Here's what I said:

'Yes, I'm really pleased to hear you're so busy! But if you *were* able to squeeze me in at some point during the whole lunchtime period, what sort of time would be the easiest for you?'

'Well, about 1.30 p.m. would probably be the easiest,' I was told.

'That's absolutely fine. Thank you very much,' I said. 'Put me down for then and we'll see you on Sunday.'

Mission accomplished! But why did this work? It's very simple, actually. I asked a question that changed the listener's focus. From focusing on the negative of how full they were, I got them to apply their thinking to a positive issue, namely when would be the easiest time to fit me in.

Does this work all the time? Of course not, but it does work 'some of the time'. Try it.

The 'How *can* we/you...?' technique

My wife acts with, and directs, a local amateur drama group she belongs to. At a recent meeting at our home to discuss how many nights the cast would perform their next dramatic 'masterpiece', some strong views were expressed. My wife was pushing for four nights, whilst others said, 'We can't do four nights because...' After some heated and extremely dramatic debate, my wife lost the argument, and the decision was taken to present the play for just three nights. Rather irritated by this, my wife sounded off to me in the kitchen where I was trying to keep a low profile!

With fire in her eyes, she told me the tale. Now, not wanting my wife in a bad mood, I suggested she change the question and try out my 'How *can* we...?' technique. I told her what I had in mind and here's what happened next. She went back into the meeting and said,

'This decision about the number of nights – I'm still not really happy about it. Let me ask you this: if we *were* going to run the show for four nights, how *could* we make that happen? How can we overcome the problems you raised before?'

Instantly, one of the people who had been opposed to her earlier suggestion said, 'Well, we *could*...' A solution was found, and the show is now planned for the four nights my wife wanted.

This technique works because the question **'How *can* we/you...?'** changes the focus of thinking, and encourages solutions, not objections. You'll be amazed at how often it works.

Let's have a look at some of those earlier negative responses to see if it's possible to apply the techniques to them.

'No, we can't get the delivery to you by then – we're just rushed off our feet at the moment.'

Try:

? **If you were able to organize something for us to make sure we got the delivery in time, when would that be?**

Or

? **How can you restructure your schedule to be able to help?**

'No, that's our lowest price. We can't go any lower.'

You could try:

? **If you were able to make some sort of gesture for us on price, even by just a small amount, what sort of deal could you do?**

Or

? **How are you able to package the deal internally to be able to get our business?**

'The computer system won't allow that, so we can't do it.'

To this, I have successfully used the following response:

? **How are you able to work around it, even if you have to do things manually?**

Again, it won't always work, but it will some of the time. Try it for yourself and see!

How can I find out?

Maybe you've asked an important question and received *'I don't know'* as the answer. This can leave you frustrated – in a 'no-man's-land' and not knowing what to do next. Instead of simply giving up at this stage, try a different question:

> **?** **I wonder if you can help me to find out...**

A close relative of mine was in hospital recently and we were sitting by his bedside waiting for the doctors to do their rounds so we could find out what the next stage in his treatment and care would be. Eventually, they came and we were told that it would have to be the consultant surgeon's decision as to whether surgery was required and what exactly this would entail.

'He's going to visit you later today,' we were told.

'Do you know when this will be?' I asked.

'No idea – just later. It could be any time at all,' was the response.

Having sat and waited another hour making polite but pointless small talk with my relative, I thought I'd have another go. This time I went to the ward sister and asked,

'Do you know when the consultant surgeon is going to be on the ward?'

'I don't know,' she said. 'It could be any time.'

This is ridiculous, I thought. Here I am, a self-styled, so-called 'question master', and I can't even get a simple answer to a simple question! I thought I'd try a different approach, so this time I asked a 'How can I find out...?' question. So I approached the ward sister again, with a smile, and said,

'Forgive me for being a pain. I know you've just told me you don't know when the consultant surgeon will be coming in, but I wonder how we might find out about his plans for the day?'

Note, not only did I pre-frame the question with an apology trigger to make her more receptive, I also used the word 'we' to make it her problem as well, and shifted the focus of the question to how we could find out.

'Well, I could speak to his secretary for you. She should know what he's doing.'

Five minutes later she came and told us that she had spoken to his secretary, and that he had just left his last engagement, and was planning to be back on the ward here at 3.45 p.m.

Job done!

Asking how you can find out is a powerful tool.

'Judge a person by their questions, rather than their answers.'

François-Marie Arouet (Voltaire),
French enlightenment writer, essayist and
philosopher (1694–1778)

Answer a question with a question

The moment you ask a question *you* take control of the conversation. This is one of the keys to questioning success. By being in control of the conversation, you maximize your chances of creating the level of influence you need to get the response you want. Why? Because your question forces the other person to *focus* on giving a response.

The way we are programmed – remember, I'm trying to avoid getting too heavy – means that a question almost compels the human brain to seek a response. Think about it – it's actually quite difficult *not* to answer when someone asks you a direct question. Understanding this, and using it, means that you can plan a series of questions to direct a person towards the outcome you're after. A good example of this technique is answering a question with another question. Suppose you're trying to sell goods or services and you are asked by your potential client or customer,

'Are you able to cope with a large volume of business in a short period of time?'

Because your prospect has asked the question, they are in control of the conversation. You also have the uncertainty of not knowing precisely how to answer. So what you need to do is take back control of the dialogue. It's easily done! Simply respond with another question:

? Do you mind me asking, what exactly do you mean by large volumes in a short period of time?

This is a very important and powerful question. On a strategic level your question has put you back in control and, as a result, you will most likely gain more information to enable you to frame a proper answer.

Ironically, I found myself using exactly this technique in my first meeting with the publishers of this book.

'When do you think you will be able to complete it?' asked the commissioning editor.

'Well, when would you like it done by?' I countered.

We both smiled. She knew what I was up to!

Make someone more receptive to your question

When you ask someone a question, what sort of state do you want them in? Ideally, they should be receptive and willing to hear what you have to say – the better their state, the more likely you are to get the response you want.

The mind is a strange thing and, as humans, most of us are pre-conditioned to respond in certain ways to certain communication triggers. All you have to do is know what these are and realize that sometimes these will soften people up and influence them to feel what you want them to feel and respond as you would like.

The purpose of this information, then, is to introduce you to a set of simple 'softeners and triggers' that will help get people into the right state so you can then ask your question. Any one of these will help you get the response you want, but note, although it's possible for you to use several in the same question or dialogue, you don't have to use them all in any one situation. They are all merely tools at your disposal and this book is the toolbag. Simply pick the one out that suits the situation best, and which you feel most comfortable with.

Here are some of my personal favourite 'softeners and triggers':

- asking for help
- apologizing first
- pre-framing your question with 'I know...'
- asking for permission

Let's look at them one by one.

Ask for help

Assuming you are in a safe and secure context and you are asked:

? **Excuse me. I wonder if you can help me?**
? **Would you mind doing me a favour?**
? **Would you mind helping me with something?**

What would be your instinctive response? Isn't it true that, in most cases, you would find yourself compelled to say, sometimes without much thought and almost automatically,

'Of course! If I can!'

'What do you need?'

'I'll do my best.'

Questions such as these put the person who is being asked the question into an instinctive state to be helpful. Isn't it obvious that a person in such a state is more likely to give you a positive response when you eventually get to what it is that you want?

So whatever you *do* want, consider prefacing your request with a question that asks for their help or assistance.

Apologize first

As with the previous trigger, putting the person you are asking in the right state to be helpful and even sympathetic to you is a good way of commencing the question process. Another way of doing this is to open your communication with an apology of some sort. (Remember what we are looking at here are those semi-automatic responses and feelings that are generated by certain communications.)

If someone were to say to you, for example:

? I'm sorry to be a pain! I wonder if I could ask you something?
? I'm really sorry to disturb you, but do you mind if ask you a question?

How would you respond? I bet in the majority of situations you'd find yourself saying something like:

'No problem! Fire away!'

'That's OK. What do you want to ask?

Of course, prefacing a question this way doesn't by itself guarantee you'll get the result you're after, but it will begin the process of getting the other person warmed up appropriately for your question.

Pre-frame your question with 'I know...'

I know I said I wouldn't keep using linguistic jargon, but 'pre-framing' is a phrase I really want you to learn and to understand. From a practical point of view, I regard this as beginning a piece of communication by stating that *you* know or understand how someone may feel about what you are about to say or ask.

This normally has the effect of making people more accepting of what you are about to ask, or even more sympathetic to a particular question. Again, this is tremendously helpful in putting them into a more receptive frame of mind to consider your request.

For example, suppose you are trying to sell something, and your potential customer blurts out,

'Can I have it cheaper?'

How do you react and feel? On the other hand, suppose they pre-framed and asked,

'I know this may sound a bit cheeky, but...'.

Wouldn't your instinct be to feel a little more sympathetic?

Here are some more examples of pre-framing:

? I know this may sound like an odd question, but...
? I know this might appear a bit blunt, but...
? I know you've already answered this question once, but...

Pre framing makes people more accepting of the odd question, the blunt question and even the repetitive request. Use of the 'I know' phrase, for example, will trigger an automatic and almost instinctive response in someone to receive your question positively.

Oh, and by the way, look back at the first line of this section:

I know I said I wouldn't keep using linguistic jargon, but 'pre-framing' is a phrase I really want you to learn and to understand.

Can you see what I've done there?

Get permission first

Another way of getting someone into a more receptive state for your question is simply to first get their permission to ask one.

Consider asking:

? Do you mind if I ask you a question?
? Do you mind if I ask you to tell me...?
? I hope you won't object to telling me about...?

Ask 'choice' questions

If you ask a question and then offer two choices, in most cases people almost feel compelled to choose from the two on offer. There are various ways you can use this to your advantage in order to get the response you want. Think of them as 'choice techniques'.

Let's look at some of them now.

The 'feel good' or 'no hassle' technique

One way is to pose your question offering two choices, but framing one of them in language that, if chosen, will enable the person to either 'feel good' or 'avoid hassle'. The result is that, in most cases, they choose the option you want them to choose, and they feel pleased about it.

> My son was running a three-day charity fundraising drama workshop in aid of the Alzheimer's Association. Parents could pay £25 to send their budding acting offspring on this workshop during the half-term holidays.
>
> After the first very successful day, one of the kids had to drop out because of some minor illness, and my son was approached by the child's mother for a refund of the fee. My son knew about this particular 'choice technique', and he used it to great effect. He said,
>
> 'I'm really sorry your son won't be coming – he'll be very disappointed. He was doing really well. As far as the refund is concerned, of course he has already done one day so I can't offer a total refund, [*here comes the 'feel good' choice question*] but I can offer you either two-thirds back or, if you're really feeling generous, you could continue to allow the money to go to the Alzheimer's Association – a very worthy cause. Which would you like to do?'
>
> Not surprisingly, she declined to ask for the money back and the charity didn't lose out.

This was a particularly good use of the technique as either choice gave her benefits. She either got her money back, or she got to feel good about giving.

Here's another example in a business selling situation:

A client of mine – a legal practice – regularly receives telephone calls asking to know its fees for carrying out a particular type of routine property transaction. As part of the process, the legal firm is responsible for ensuring that something called the Stamp Duty Land Tax Form is completed. The customer can either do this themselves or pay extra to have my client do it for them. They were having difficulty getting customers to opt to pay for this service until I showed them the 'no hassle' technique.

Now the person dealing with the enquiry and giving the fee says,

'Of course you could save £75 on our fees by dealing with the form yourself [*choice 1*], or, if you feel uncomfortable about wading through seven pages of time-consuming complex tax forms and material, which has to be spot-on, we could do it for you [*choice 2*]. Which would you prefer?'

Guess which most people pick?

Ask 'alternative positives'

I have a confession to make. This is one of my own personal favourites, and I challenge those who deal with me after they read this book to identify when I'm using it. Believe me – it won't be difficult to spot!

All you have to do is ask a question that gives a limited number of choices to consider. Most people simply then choose from those options on offer. At its very simplest, to prove the point to any cynics reading this book, think about what happens in a restaurant. If you are offered a choice of three possible starters, what do you do? You choose one of them! Nobody actually says you can't ask for something else, but most people feel compelled to focus on and choose from the options put in front of them.

Go to a business meeting and you will often be asked,

'Tea or coffee?'

What do you do? Mostly you will accept one or the other. I bet you don't turn around and say,

'Can I possibly have a hot chocolate, please?'

So how can you use this notion in your personal or business life to get the sort of response you want? Simple! Ask questions that narrow down the options and people will go for one or the other. You could even extend the technique to a sequence of questions. Once the person being asked has chosen one of the options, ask yet another 'alternative positive' question (with choices) and you are gradually steering them towards the response you wanted all along.

One of the reasons why this is so effective is because, if you do it well, you are making the other person feel that they are in control. Imagine you are in a business situation, and someone calls you to ask your fees. At some point in the communication you will, of course, give the information they are requesting. However, at the moment the question is put, immediately ask:

? **When would be a good time to do the job? Are you looking for it sooner or later?**

(Note you have diverted the focus from price to timescale.)

If they answer 'sooner', offer them more options:

? **Today or tomorrow? This week or next week? Morning or afternoon?**

If they answer 'Later', again offer them more options:

? **OK. Is it better for you at the end of this month or next month?**

The wide choice technique

There are occasions in both your personal and business life where it can be useful to allow others to choose from a wide list of options. However, the trick is to phrase the question in such a way as to limit the responses to those that would be good for you.

For example, perhaps you have spoken at a presentation or a seminar and been on the receiving end of delegate feedback? Suppose, instead of asking on your feedback sheet for general comments, you ask,

? **What are the three most valuable things you have learnt during the seminar?**

What happens? Virtually everyone in the room will sit for a couple of minutes and focus positively on the three things that they are going to put down.

Avoid multiple negative choices!

If you're going to offer people 'choice' questions as a way of influencing them, don't offer them two negative choices. If you do, then don't be disappointed or surprised when they don't choose something that gives you a positive result.

> I know someone who attended a job interview and, after a week, had not heard anything. Eventually he rang up and asked,
>
> 'Is the reason I haven't heard from you because you either don't like me, or you've found someone else who has more experience than me?'

I've also had salespeople offer me negative options. After being given a price I've been asked,

> 'Is that too expensive for you, or are you not able to make your mind up now?'

To summarize then:

Ask a question offering positive alternative choices

Out of interest, which two techniques or tips that you have read so far in the book have you found most helpful? List them below:

1) ....………..

2) ..…..   ....………..

Did it work? If you have actually come up with two choices, then the technique did work!

Get people to ask you what you want them to ask

How often have you been in some sort of social or business networking situation where you want the people you are mixing with to ask *you* certain questions? Maybe you want them to ask you for your business card, or to ask what you do for a living? Essentially, you want them to do this because it will open up the conversation and give you a platform to talk about what you want.

Here is one of the simplest and most effective ways to achieve this:

If you want someone to ask you a question, ask them the same question first!

This is another classic example of 'influence'. Ask somebody a particular question and, more often than not, it almost compels them, sometimes unconsciously, to ask the same question back.

The most obvious example of this, which you probably ask every day, is the question,

'How are you?'

Invariably, back will come the response,

'I'm fine! How about you?'

You have made that person ask you a question simply by asking it to them first. It's such an automatic response that sometimes people will say, 'I'm fine!' before you've even asked them! Have you ever had that experience?

You can extend this simple technique to many business and social situations. Suppose you want someone to know what you do. Ask *them*,

'What do you do for a living?'

Invariably, back will come an answer such as,

'I'm an architect. And you?'

Suppose you want the person to whom you are talking to know who you work for. Simply ask them which company *they* work for. Their response might be, for example,

'I'm with Juicy Grapefruit plc.'

They might tell you more by saying,

'I'm the operations director at Juicy Grapefruit plc.'

The important bit, though, is that in most cases they'll go on to ask,

'How about you? Who are you with?'

This will be your opportunity to tell them you are the marketing director at Automated Fruit Pickers Ltd.

Suppose you want someone to ask for your card. Now you know what to do – simply ask for theirs!

If you want to chat about the great holiday you're going on, ask them casually,

'Any holiday plans?'

They'll answer, and then ask you,

'What about you?'

You can now tell them about your charity fundraising trip up Everest with an ironing board and a piano, and ask them for sponsorship!

If you want to talk to someone about a topic ask them about it first!

'Who questions much, shall learn much, and retain much.'
Sir Francis Bacon, English author, courtier and philosopher (1561–1626)

Ask a 'because' question

Before we get to this technique I'd like to ask you a question:

?   **Can you make sure you set aside at least ten minutes without
interruptions to read this, because ten minutes is a particularly
effective time to spend on it?**

Have a look back at the question I've just asked before we go on.
Read it again and again. Yes, actually the question is nonsense! Did you
pick up on the fact that it doesn't really mean anything? Why is ten
minutes particularly effective? What if you had spent nine minutes on
it? Does that mean those nine minutes wouldn't count?

Look back at the question yet again. The key word in the question
is **'because'**. To understand this technique you need to know that the
simple use of this word will often trigger an unconscious reaction in
someone to believe that there is a *reason* why they are being asked to do
something. Most of us have an automatic reflex to say 'yes' or to behave
in a specific way if there is a reason.

Believe it or not, even if the reason given is a poor one, or even
nonsense, use of the word 'because' will still trigger the positive 'yes'
reflex, and very often you'll get the response you want. In fact, sometimes
the people you're asking won't even hear the actual reason itself. They'll
hear 'because' and their unconscious mind immediately tells them, 'Hey
– there's a reason! I'll say yes.'

Don't believe me? Think I've really lost it?

Try it. Have some fun!

Ask something of someone, but include the word 'because' in the
question, followed by a reason, and you'll dramatically increase the 'yes'
responses.

Think back again to my question at the opening of this section. I'll
bet many of you missed the fact that the question didn't really mean
anything, and actually felt you needed to devote ten minutes to this
couple of pages. If you did, then the word 'because' was the trigger for
that reaction.

Let me give you another simple example of the effectiveness of this
technique:

Arriving at a very busy car park recently there was a big sign up
saying 'FULL'. The yellow-coated car park attendant was turning

people away with an authoritative wave. My frustrated passengers immediately commented that we'd have to find somewhere else to park, and so would be late.

'No,' I said. 'He'll let us in. Let's try the magic word "because".'

So I ignored the madly waving arm and drove up to him. I opened my window and said very nicely,

'I know it says "FULL", but is there any way you can find us a space *because* it's a problem parking somewhere else?' (I emphasized the word 'because'.)

Without saying a word he just lifted up the barrier and let us in!

Now I know what you're thinking … that's unbelievable … what kind of black magic is this? Astonishing as it may seem, however, whilst it doesn't work all the time, a question containing the word 'because' does produce a positive result with a high degree of frequency. Try it and let me know about your successes.

'Question everything. Learn something.
Answer nothing.'

Engineers' motto

? 83

Get a better price just by asking!

Everyone likes a bargain! Well here's the good news. You don't have to wait until the January sales to stand a chance of getting a good deal. As I've already said earlier in the book, all you need to do is 'just ask' for one. What's the worst that can happen? You'll get a 'no' and the price stays the same, and you can still decide whether to buy or not to buy. What's the best that can happen? You'll get a bargain!

Whether you're buying things in a shop, test-driving a car or booking a holiday or hotel over the phone, if you ask in an appropriate way you *will*, sometimes, get the response you are hoping for.

The same applies if you're in business. From time to time you will need to buy advertising or exhibition space, professional services or stock. Again, simply asking for a better deal will, in the long run, potentially leave you with more cash. The big question is, *how* do you ask?

Let me give you a few suggestions and then tell you what they all have in common.

? Is there anything you can do for me on price, because I would really appreciate it?

? If I were to go ahead now, what's the best deal you can do for me?

? I'm sorry – I can't say yes at that price because I have a budget. How close can you get to it for me?

? How much discount can you give me if I buy more than one?

? How much discount are you able to give because I'm an existing customer?

These questions all have something in common in that they employ one of two techniques. They either offer a benefit to the other person in return for giving a discount, or give a reason why you're asking. Look back at them again now and identify these attributes. My experience and personal experimentation has shown that use of one or both of these techniques will have an unconscious influence over the person you are asking and, in the long run, increase your success rate.

Note that your tone is important, too. Don't be confrontational or pushy. The tone you are looking for is sincere, calm, friendly and confidently appreciative. Ask the question as though you have a real problem over the price, and are expecting the answer to be positive.

The other question you might try, particularly if you are buying services, is:

? **How expensive will the work be?**

This question draws others into the same price trap that you would fall into if you were asked the same question. Isn't it the case that if you were asked how much something was going to be, you would often automatically reach for a low price?

Framing the question with the word 'expensive' in it shifts the person's focus to the expense as being of real concern. Even if you don't feel comfortable asking for a better deal it will maximize your chances of getting a good figure from the outset.

So if you want the January sales all year round, 'just ask' for a better deal!

Ask a question that prompts the answer you want

There's an extremely easy, yet effective, way of asking questions that instantly alters the focus of the person you are talking to. At the very least, it makes it harder for them to turn you down. All you need to do is to ask a question that, in effect, 'jumps' a stage, and actually presupposes that you have already had a positive response. Suppose you wanted to meet someone to discuss future business potential. You could ask them, 'Do you want to meet to discuss this?'

This question, however, offers two choices to the person you are asking – 'yes' or 'no' – and their focus is definitely on these two options.

However, you could simply 'jump' a stage and presuppose they *do* want to meet you. You could ask:

? **When are you free to meet to talk this through?**

In this example, the fact that they do want to meet you has been pre-supposed, and the focus has simply been shifted on to arrangements over when this might happen. You could couple this technique with the one I mentioned in 'alternative positives' (page 77) and add:

? **When are you free to meet to talk this through? Later this week? Or is next week better for you?**

This technique is incredibly powerful in sales as well. Imagine you are in the process of selling something. You've been asked the price and have given it. Instead of asking them, 'Would you like to go ahead?', you could ask:

? **How many would you like?**
? **What's the best time for you to come and pick it up?**
? **When would you like it to be delivered?**

Remember, asking a question that prompts the answer you want will increase your chances of getting it!

Don't frame your questions negatively

Some people are so embarrassed to ask for something that they pose their question in a negative way. This not only makes it easier for a person to say 'no' – it also almost impels them towards a negative answer.

I was walking through a shopping centre recently, when I was approached by someone who said to me,

'I don't suppose you could spare me five minutes for a survey?'

The question made it easy for me to reply,

'I'm sorry. No, I can't.'

On a train recently, the refreshments person pushing a trolley up the aisle was saying,

'I don't suppose you want any refreshments? You don't want any, do you sir?'

The bottom line is that a positive question will always score over a negative one.

Suppose our characters above had said:

? Excuse me. I know it's a bit of a pain, [aligning with someone is always a good idea] but can you spare me a quick five minutes to help with a survey? That would be really appreciated.

Or, in the train example, even a simple list of positive choices would have been better than the negative question that was used. For example:

? Teas? Coffees? Nice cold refreshments?

The key is to pose your question in such a way as to almost make the person you are asking *want* to say 'yes'.

How much time do you have?

Remembering to ask this question, which you can put either to yourself or to others, has the potential to help you in one of two possible ways. It could help you to maximize your performance and results in business meetings, and it could simply save you massive amounts of time.

Let me ask you this. Have you ever been in a business meeting where you've eased into it with a bit of small talk and a coffee, only to learn that the person you're seeing, whom you want to ask for something, has to leave in ten minutes? You then feel under pressure to get to your question, and may end up failing to frame it in quite the way you had hoped.

Perhaps you've experienced a similar situation, where the person you're talking to expects more time from you than you want to give?

Asking someone:

? **How much time do you have?**

can be a very important tactic. If somebody has agreed to meet me, I would normally ask right at the beginning of the meeting, as a matter of routine, with a smile on my face:

? **Listen, thanks very much for seeing me. So that I don't overstay my welcome, can I just ask how much time you're OK for?**

If it's me who has agreed to see someone, I might ask at the outset:

? **Thanks very much for coming in. I don't know how you're fixed, but I'm OK for the next half hour before my next engagement. Is that going to be all right for you?**

These sorts of questions facilitate efficient and positive business results and output.

Ask questions that give praise and build rapport

Genuine praise and compliments are always appreciated and, provided they're given sincerely and in context, they are a great tool for building rapport:

? **Have you any idea just how good your paintings are?**
? **Do you realize how effective you were in that business meeting earlier today?**
? **Where did you learn to do that? It was just fantastic!**

You could, of course, simply *tell* somebody something positive about themselves. However, when you frame it as a question you influence them into giving a proper response, which invariably leads to a positive conversation about 'them' – a conversation that you control. Even if they pretend to be embarrassed, the exchange will make most people feel good.

Think about it for a second. Imagine that you hear someone play the piano, and you go over to them and tell them,

'That was very good!'

What is their response going to be? It will probably be limited to a smile and a...

'Thank you very much.'

And that is likely to be the end of the conversation.

However, what if you give your praise as a question? Suppose you say, instead:

? **How long have you been playing the piano? It sounds as though you've been doing it for years.**

Their likely response will be something along the lines of...

'Well, I have been playing it for years!'

or:

'No, I've only been playing for a couple of years.'

Either way, you are into a positive conversation of which you are in control. This conversation will enable you to build rapport.

Let me give you an example of how this very simple technique was turned into cash!

I once encountered a magician who ran magic shows in restaurants for children, leaving the adults to eat in peace. He told me that, unlike the waiters, he hardly ever got any tips. One day, however, he accidentally hit on the 'ask a question that gives praise' technique. If a child was particularly well behaved, he would make a point of asking the parents,

'Do you know how well behaved your son is?'

Because it was framed as a question, a mini-conversation would follow and, invariably, so would a decent tip!

**So next time you want to praise someone
or give them a compliment,
ask yourself how you can do it as a question.**

'He who knows all the answers has not yet been asked all the questions.'

Source unknown

Invite yourself into a conversation

If you're in business, how do you receive telephone calls from people who want to know your price for various things? If...

'Can I have a quote for such-and-such a thing?'

is a regular question, you'll know the danger of becoming trapped in a dialogue that revolves exclusively around your price.

There's a simple question technique I use to deal with these sorts of questions. I call it the 'invite yourself into the conversation' technique.

Just think for a moment about what you are trying to do, and why. Your aim at the beginning of any such conversation is to take control of the call, show your personal interest in the caller and build rapport so that the caller feels comfortable about answering your questions. If it's a possible sales situation, you're probably also hoping to differentiate yourself from your competition on something other than price.

Here, then, is how you invite yourself into a conversation, which achieves all these things. Imagine, for example, that your phone rings and the caller asks,

'I wonder if you can tell me how much you charge to tune a piano?'

You could, of course, simply reply,

'We charge £45,'

and leave it at that, knowing that the caller will now ring a couple of other tuners to see who is the cheapest. However, suppose you said in a warm and friendly tone:

? 'No problem at all. I'm more than happy to explain how our charges work. But, before we get into the figures, can I just check that you're OK for a couple of minutes so I can get a bit of background about what sort of piano you have, when you might want it doing, and any other relevant details? That way I can make sure I give you the best possible figure I can? Is that OK?'

By asking this question you have taken control of the conversation.

Remember – whoever asks the questions controls the conversation!

You've demonstrated your interest in the caller by showing you want to know more about their requirements; have got permission to ask other questions that will give you the chance to build up a bit of rapport and have differentiated yourself from others they ring, who simply snap out a price. All this can be achieved in just a few short seconds, in a way that makes it look like it's all for their benefit.

By the way, you don't need to wait for a price inquiry to use this technique. If you have to give practical advice or help to customers or clients at work, you can use the same approach.

You may even find it works in personal situations, too. Suppose a friend or a member of your family has called you. They are a bit upset about something that has happened to them and they want to unload their tale of woe on you and get your support and advice. It's quite likely that you would end up listening to a long-winded and disjointed torrent of emotional upset, without really being able to piece together exactly what has happened. Well, this is where you might employ the 'invite yourself into a conversation' technique. You could try saying the following:

> **?** 'Listen I can hear you're really upset, and I'm more than happy to give you time to get it all out, but before you launch into the whole tale can I take a few minutes just to understand what has happened? It would be good to find out exactly how you are, and to ask a few other questions so when we start to talk the problem through I'm in the best possible position to help. Is that OK?'

If you read this book and have an issue or question, and contact me about it, don't be surprised if you hear me use this technique on you!

Sow seeds of doubt

Have you ever been in a situation where, in your opinion, someone you care about is on the point of making a bad decision? Maybe, for example, one of your offspring is planning to drop out of university tomorrow because of work pressure, in order to take a six months' sabbatical riding rollercoasters in Florida theme parks!

If you are in business, have you ever encountered potential clients or customers who say,

'I've had a cheaper quote from somewhere else.'

or,

'You're a bit higher on price than others I have spoken to.'?

I'm quite confident that every one of us has experienced a situation, whether business or personal, where it would have been wonderful to have had a strategy to get someone to reconsider their position without an argument. The truth, for most of us, is that when we want to get someone to think again or see a different point of view, we simply argue by taking an opposing position. For example:

'Drop out of university to go to Florida for six months? You must be mad!'

'We like to think we're very competitive. Anyway, if you go for the cheapest, don't be surprised if you get bottom-of-the-barrel service!'

Wouldn't it be better if, without arguing, or even telling someone that you think they're wrong, you had a technique that made them rethink the situation for themselves, in a way that exerted some common-sense pressure on them to see things your way?

Next time you find yourself in this sort of situation, you'll have a technique to hand. All you have to do is say to yourself:

SSOD it!

(Don't say this out loud, by the way, or you might not get the exactly the reaction you want!)

If you haven't guessed it yet, **SSOD™** is an acronym. It stands for:

S = sow
S = seeds
O = of
D = doubt

All you have to do is ask questions that will prompt the person you're asking to give responses that will 'sow seeds of doubt' in their own mind about the course of action they are considering.

So how do you use this technique? Well, you need to do three simple things:

◆ **Align with their position.** Say something that shows you see it from their point of view. If they are expecting an argument, this will wrong-foot them to begin with.

◆ **Tell them you are going to ask questions.** Actually announce that you are going to ask them a few questions, which will help them definitely make their minds up.

◆ **Ask them 'SSOD™ it' questions.** Pose a series of questions that you know will sow seeds of doubt in their mind. The best types of questions to ask are those to which they have to respond, 'I don't know' or 'no'.

Let's look at our two examples again, bearing the techniques I've just listed in mind.

In the first situation, you might respond as follows:

'You know what? I can totally understand why you might be feeling the pressure. Three essays at the same time does seem unfair [*align*]. But, let me ask you a few questions that will help you make your mind up once and for all about whether it's the right thing to do [*tell them you are going to ask questions*]. If you leave for Florida tomorrow, where will you stay? How will you finance the trip? Are you allowed to work? Will the university have you back in the future? Have you discussed this with your tutors and friends? Can you be certain you won't regret it in a few weeks' time when it's too late? Do you think it's wise to make long-term decisions based on an immediate, short-term issue? [*Ask 'SSOD™ it' questions and let them answer each one before going on to the next.*]'

In the second situation, you could use the technique to overcome price-related obstacles in sales situations by saying:

'You know what? If I were in your shoes, I could see why you might be tempted to go with someone who's a bit cheaper [*align*]. But just let me ask you a few questions, which will help you decide whether you're making the right decision or not [*tell them you are going to ask questions*]. When you spoke to the other company, did you find out exactly who would be carrying out your work? Did they include such-and-such in the price? Did you find out how experienced they were at jobs like this? Do they understand the timescales we discussed, and your personal circumstances, or did you just get a price? [*Ask them 'SSOD™ it' questions and let them answer before going on to the next.*]'

Think it through carefully and ask these sorts of questions. The more 'nos' and 'don't knows' you get, the better! The more likely the other person will be to reprocess their thinking and come up with the outcome that you want. Remember:

If you want to influence someone to your way of thinking, ask 'SSOD™ it' questions!

'He who asks a question is a fool for five minutes; he who does not ask a question remains a fool forever.'

Chinese proverb

Ask for the business

Endless books and articles have been written on this subject. In fact, when I typed 'close the sale' into an internet search engine, I found more than 155,000,000 possibilities offered for my reading pleasure! For this precise reason, I am now going to write the shortest text on the subject in the history of personal and business development books, and give you the simplest and most obvious advice of all:

**If you're in a selling situation and
you don't actually ask outright for the business,
don't be surprised if you don't get it.**

Don't 'if' your potential customer or client. I have come across too many people in sales situations who say,

'Well, *if* you'd like to go ahead, please don't hesitate to come back to us. We'd be delighted to help.'

Be specific and simply ask outright:

?   Well, we'd really love to do some business with you. Can I take it you'd like to progress things with us?

Ask questions which make it easy for someone to say 'yes'

The other day my wife asked me to pop out and post a letter.

'It'll only take you a few minutes and the fresh air will do you good, You've been at the computer all day!' she sensibly suggested.

I agreed. After all, I like to be helpful, and how long could it possibly take?

'Actually, if you're going out to post a letter, would you mind doing it at the post office in the mini-supermarket because we could do with a loaf of bread?' she added.

As I was picking up the loaf of bread in the shop, my mobile phone rang. Guess who?

'I've been making a list,' said my wife. 'Whilst you're there, could you get a few other things we need?'

Forty minutes later I was still at the checkout behind four other people, with a trolley-load of shopping, trying to convince myself that it's good to be helpful and that I was at least getting some fresh air! As I hauled the eight back-breaking bags of shopping into my car, my mobile phone rang again. Who could it possibly be?

'Can you do me a little favour on your way home? It won't take long, and you're going that way anyway. Could you stop off at Harry's and collect something that we need for the meeting this evening?'

Finally, after an hour and a half, I was back at my desk at home – overdosed on fresh air, and feeling smug about how helpful I had been!

The moral of this story is very simple in the context of this book. If you want to ask for something, consciously consider asking for a 'small' something first that makes it easy for the other person to say 'yes'. This technique can make it easier for you to ask and, potentially, almost impossible for the other person to turn you down.

From a technique point of view, the question you should be asking yourself is:

What can I ask that will make it easy for the other person to say 'yes'?

In business, of course, this technique is hugely valuable and is used every day. Suppose you are in discussion with a customer or an organization that you would like to do regular business with. A simple approach might be to 'just ask' them if they would like to try you out at a special rate.

For example:

> **?** I appreciate we may be a little more expensive than one or two other firms, but how would it be if we were to take on a couple of initial jobs for you at a special trial figure of £x? This way, you'll be able to see for yourself why we charge a little more. Either you'll be so pleased you gave us the chance and want to carry on at our standard rate, or at that stage you can try one of the lower-charging firms. Either way you can't lose. Can we progress things on that basis?

If you think you are above this technique, I can guarantee you have been on the receiving end of it regularly! When a supermarket persuades you to 'buy one and get one free' they are using this technique on you. All they are doing is asking a question that makes it easy for you to say 'yes'.

Would it be helpful if...?

Would it be helpful to have a technique that almost locked the person you are asking into giving 'yes' as an answer? (If you have just answered 'yes' to this question, then you have just experienced a successful demonstration of the method!)

Essentially, all you have to do is ask **'Would it be helpful if...?'** followed by something that you know with reasonable certainty would be. It almost follows that you will get a 'yes' response. This might be sufficient in its own right, or it might be the platform for other questions.

Let me try some more on you:

Would it be helpful if...
? ... I could show you how to lose weight and keep it off?
? ... I could improve your golf swing?
? ... I could save you money on your holiday this year?
? ... I were to pop in to explain how the product works?
? ... I were to give you a few suggestions about how to deal with that personal problem?

Look carefully at these. You will find the answer to all of them is likely to be 'yes'. Next time you want to ask somebody for something, consider how you could phrase your question with a 'Would it be helpful if...?' introduction.

> Just before giving a series of radio interviews some years ago, I contacted the programme's production team and said,
>
> 'I know how busy you and the interviewer are. Would it be helpful if I sent through three or four suggestions of questions you might want to ask me?'
>
> They were grateful for the offer and agreed. The result was, of course, that it made the interview easier for both of us.

What do I have to do to change your mind?

However carefully you read this book and practise and perfect the techniques, there will still be situations where, no matter what you do, the answer is still 'no'. I have one final, catch-all technique, which occasionally turns things around and produces the result you are after.

Simply try asking:

?   What do I have to do to change your mind and get you to say 'yes'?

Sometimes they will tell you exactly what you need to do, and the ball is at least back in your court.

'A prudent question is one-half of wisdom.'
Sir Francis Bacon, English author, courtier and philosopher (1561–1626)

How should you ask?

If you want to make something happen, and you have decided you are going to 'just ask', a simple but very important initial question is **'How should you ask?'** This question is important in its own right, so consciously take your time thinking about it. The only real answer to it is, whichever method is likely to get you the best result!

In some circumstances, all options might be open to you and you could see the person face to face, telephone them or write to them in a traditional letter or via email. Let me give you some guidance, however, based on my experience. As a rule of thumb, in most circumstances, I would choose a face-to-face or over-the-phone approach over a written one. Let me give you a number of reasons why.

- Firstly, in many situations, but particularly in business, most people make their initial approach in writing. A non-written and personal approach, however, if done appropriately and sensitively, differentiates you from the rest so you stand out.
- Secondly, once you send a letter or email, you have no control over exactly how it is processed. You could write to one carefully selected person, only to get a reply from someone else based on a computer-generated standard response. A skilful person asking the question face to face or over the phone, using some of the techniques in this book, has a much greater chance of being able to build rapport, engage the person in a conversation and positively influence the outcome of the call.
- And thirdly, if you ask a question over the phone or in person, it is possible that, although you might not get exactly what you're after, you might still come away with other secondary information that is useful to you.

There are only three situations when I would write first:

- when I simply can't get access to the person directly;
- when I'm told that my approach *must* be in writing;
- when I want to ask so many people that a personal approach is practically impossible.

However, it's important in the context of this book to understand that if you do decide to 'just ask', most of the techniques I've described in

? 101

the **'Technology of Questions**™**'** section can also be applied when asking in writing. For example, if you're emailing someone in order to set up a meeting with them, don't ask them *'if'* they want to meet, but instead *'when'* might be convenient. And offer them a couple of dates. The focus is then shifted to the practical arrangements over the meeting.

If you are having problems making something happen, write and ask 'how' your request can be made to work.

'The only stupid question is the one you don't ask.'

Dr Richard Milton

It's not what you say, it's the way you say it

My focus so far in this book has been on understanding the 'just asking' mindset, and on the techniques you can use when it comes to deciding 'what' to say. Now I'd like to add to the pot a different aspect of the 'Technology of Questions™'. It's time to factor in something else: **'how'** you say it.

Here's something that may surprise you. Research indicates that for effective, influential, face-to-face communication, the actual words you choose and use account for only 7% of communication, your tone and vocal emphasis for 38%, and your physical visual factors, such as your facial expressions, body language and gestures, for a whacking 55%! For telephone communications, the figures also make interesting reading. Apparently, 84% of effective communication comes from tone, vocal emphasis, speed, volume, clarity and articulation, and only 16% from what is actually said.

If you doubt this, just think for a moment of some of your favourite comedians and television presenters. The late, great Eric Morecombe didn't need to open his mouth – he merely had to raise his glasses and his eyebrows to get a laugh! Try delivering one of Billy Connolly's stories and tirades word for word, however, and you know what? – no one will laugh. His genius is not that what he says is funny, but is almost entirely because of how he says it.

Think also of the late Steve Irwin, the Australian television presenter who picked up lethal snakes and wrestled with crocodiles. Despite his seemingly manic antics, what made him so compelling and brilliant as a presenter was not just what he said, but the positively energetic, enthusiastic, even passionate way in which he gestured and talked about the animals.

If you really want to research this area in detail for your degree in linguistics, then you are reading the wrong book. If, however, you just want a few practical tips about how you can use this information when you are asking questions to help get the desired response, then keep reading!

Without getting too scientific about this area, I can sum it all up in one word:

Rapport!

If you want to maximize your chances of getting the answer you want from the people you are asking, you need to build rapport with them. Two of the factors that help build rapport are:

- physical movements and gestures;
- vocal tone and emphasis.

What you really need to ask yourself, therefore, is:

? **How should you be speaking?**
? **What gestures should you use to build rapport with someone?**

After all, isn't it common sense that someone you have rapport with is likely to give you a more favourable response?

Let's put it a different way:

? **Are there things that you can do that will make others feel more comfortable when they deal with you?**
? **Are there things you can avoid doing, so that you don't make people feel uncomfortable?**

The practical problem when it comes to answering these two questions is that most of the things you do in terms of your voice and movements are unconscious. In other words, if you are doing something that turns people off, you probably don't know it (and no one will tell you). Other people may not realize what it is either – they just know they feel uncomfortable around you.

> I have a client. For obvious reasons I can't mention his name, but I can tell you this. If the art of making people feel uncomfortable were an Olympic event, he would be a multiple gold-medallist!
>
> Without any conscious effort on his part, he stares down at you, narrowing his cruel eyes into a grim look, mouth turned down, and spits out his conversation and questions in a confrontational, dry tone, which is somewhere between sarcasm and an accusation of murder. His head stays still, his arms and legs are crossed as he converses with people and, despite my best efforts at humour and light conversation, a smile is not part of his repertoire.

I bet he's fun at parties! The bottom line is that he's not very popular.

The scary thing is that he's probably unaware of why, and doesn't realize how his tone and gestures, or lack of them, come across to others.

So why am I telling you about this gentleman? Because, by mentioning his negatives and his problems as an extreme example, I hope that as I highlight certain categories you will look objectively in the mirror, search your conscience or even ask close family and friends about your own strengths and weaknesses.

In the rest of this section, we'll take a look at a few general tips about the vocal and physical issues that contribute to making people feel more comfortable.

'If a person is not in the habit of asking,
"What is this? What is this?"
then I cannot do anything for him.'
Confucius, Chinese philosopher and
reformer (551 BC–479 BC)

Use body language to ask for a 'yes'

As I mentioned before, your body is a tool of influence. Used in the right way it can massively assist you in your communications and rapport-building, to the extent that those you are 'just asking' feel more comfortable with you, and therefore are more likely to respond positively to your requests.

When thinking of your body as a way of helping you get positive responses, try thinking of my acronym '**SHLEPS**™'. It stands for:

S = smile
H = hands and head
L = laugh
E = eyes
P = personal space
S = shakes

Whilst these physical aspects are not intended to be an exhaustive list of the areas of non-verbal communication, for the purposes of brevity and practicality in the context of this book they are, as far as I'm concerned, the most significant for you to use and remember. Here, then, are a few important things to consciously consider relating to each of them.

S = smile

Here's a fact: when you smile at someone, their natural instinct is to smile back. Smiling has a positive influence on people and affects their responses to you. Ask for something with a smile on your face, or smile throughout your conversational build-up to the question, and it's harder for them to say 'no'. Their natural instinct will be to say 'yes'!

This might sound strange, but it works over the phone as well. If you smile as you talk and ask questions, somehow or other it affects your style and tone, and you almost 'transmit' your smile. Try it.

The opposite is also true. If you have a permanent scowl on your face, like my client above, don't be surprised if you get frequent negative responses.

?　Honesty question: Are you a smiler?

H = hands and head

Hands: I'm going to be very blunt in this section. If you cross or fold your arms in meetings or social situations, you will unconsciously be perceived as being negative and unfriendly. It's as if you are setting up a barrier. A strange thing will often happen: whatever pose you adopt will unconsciously be 'mirrored' by the other person, so then you'll have two people setting up barriers. Hardly an atmosphere to 'just ask' for what you want with any expectation of getting it!

However, hold your arms in an open, unfolded, relaxed position, and this will be transmitted to the other person, who is again likely to adopt the same pose. Isn't this scenario more likely to produce the result that you want?

? **Honesty question: Do you have a habit of folding your arms?**

Hand gestures: Have you ever had some form of training in speech or presentation-giving and been told not to move your hands as it is distracting? A client of mine told me recently that he had gone through some presentation-training where he had been videoed, and was told afterwards that he should try to keep his hands still.

What nonsense! Many people almost 'speak' with their hands. Gestures can inspire communication, making it seem more attractive, interesting and engaging, and can often hold attention. They are part of a person's individual style.

Don't hold back on gestures. They will make you appear more open, honest and energetic, and will add colour and emphasis to what you are saying. My tip is to be yourself.

? **Honesty question: How do you use your hands?**

Head nodding and shaking: With the exception of one or two cultures, in most cases another simple way of influencing people positively (including yourself) is to nod your head. If someone is talking to you, nodding your head indicates to them that you are interested. If you are asking someone a question, nod your head gently as you ask. It encourages a positive response.

Of course, the opposite is also true. Shaking your head whilst asking a question is sending a negative signal to the person you're dealing with. If you ask the question,

'I don't suppose you can do me a favour, can you?'

? 107

whilst shaking your head, don't be surprised if you don't get the kind of positive result you were hoping for.

? **Honesty question: Are you a head 'nodder' or a 'shaker'?**

L = laugh

Laughing has the same effect as smiling. If you find the opportunity to use appropriate humour in your meetings, or indeed something that simply lightens the tone, grasp it. When someone sees you physically laughing at something they have said or done, or you are able to make them laugh, you are on your way to building rapport with them. Essentially, laughing creates a more personal, friendly and informal situation, in which people tend to be more relaxed and you become more attractive to them. The result is that when you 'just ask' for something they will feel more inclined to say 'yes'.

? **Honesty question: How often do you laugh when dealing with people?**

E = eyes

Let's keep it simple. If you want to get on with somebody and send them positive signals, then make eye contact with them for about three-quarters of the time you are conversing with them. As an exception to this, if it's obvious that the person you are with doesn't do this, then 'mirror' their degree of eye contact or they will unconsciously feel that you are trying to intimidate them.

While we're on the subject of eyes, here's another really important tip. Don't let them wander. If you're talking to someone, give them your absolute and undivided attention. If, in the middle of them explaining something to you, they see you look up at the clock on the wall, pick up a letter and start to read it, or gaze with interest at the attractive waiter or waitress at the next table, you have broken the rapport. You may as well have said out loud that you're more interested in the time, that letter, or that person over there, than in what they are saying to you. If you then ask your question, don't be surprised if they turn you down.

? **Honesty question: Where do you look when speaking to people?**

P = personal space

Have you ever been in a business or social setting and the person you are speaking to comes just that bit too close?

I used to chair an annual three-day business networking conference, and one of the regular delegates would talk to me from a distance of about four inches away. I would instinctively back away and, guess what? He would step forward and invade my space again. He would then chase me around the room until I could escape! It made me feel very uncomfortable.

As I said before, the basic rule, if you want to get people to respond well to whatever you want to ask them, is to make them feel comfortable. To do this, remember not to get too close while you are doing the asking, unless you have a relationship with them that permits this. About three or four feet is a reasonably comfortable and safe distance.

? **Honesty question: How close do you get when talking to someone?**

S = shakes

Most social and business meetings begin and end with a handshake. You may have it in mind that you are going to ask something of the person you are meeting, so getting this right is crucial. But what *is* the most effective way of performing this gesture? You may have heard that the correct way is a 'firm' shake, but actually this is not always the case. Let me ask you a question:

? **Have you ever offered your hand to someone who squeezed it so firmly that it hurt? How did that make you feel towards them?**

Some people confuse 'firm' with 'knuckle-crushing' – not a great way to build rapport. People who do this are unconsciously trying to assert their power and dominance over you – again, not an ideal way to make oneself popular.

So what do you do?

Simple. For a fraction of a second, feel the amount of pressure that you are given and then match it. If the other person squeezes firmly, do the same. If they give you a weak shake, give them one back of the same, or less, pressure. People tend to feel more comfortable with people who are 'like' themselves.

? **Honesty question: What is your handshake like?**

? 109

Just Ask

Make sure you look
the part

Sometimes our appearance, or the way we dress, can play a part in influencing the response we might get to a question we've 'just asked'. Isn't it the case that if you are going for a job interview or business meeting, you choose to dress in a particular way? All you're really trying to do here is fit in, so that you and the person, or people, you are with will feel more comfortable.

A useful couple of questions to ask therefore are:

? **What is the appropriate dress for this situation?**
? **How do I need to dress in order to get the reaction and level of influence I am after?**

I was involved in a research experiment many years ago where I was able to put this theory to the test.

My company was retained to advise a major car dealership on the way in which its sales team dealt with customers. I was interested to see if the way customers dressed had any impact on the way they were dealt with by the sales force. The answer was that it made an enormous difference.

When I walked in looking rather scruffy in my T-shirt and old jeans, they didn't take me too seriously when I asked them for a test-drive in their top-of-the-range executive car. However, I can scrub up quite well and, when I returned sometime later wearing my three-piece, pin-striped suit, the sales team couldn't do enough to try to impress!

If you want another, very cynical and rather sexist, example of how clothes and appearance can influence people in the business world to give certain responses to questions, look no further than any major business exhibition or tradeshow. Despite the current climate of political correctness, you will still find many of the stands are run by very attractive, provocatively-dressed young women. At some shows, at which the general profile of the visitors is predominantly male, many of the companies concerned know that male delegates will find it harder to say 'no' to these ladies when asked the tradeshow questions:

? 'So what brings you here today?'
? 'Are you interested in taking a look at what we have to offer?'
? 'Would you like to stop and put your card in the box to win a bottle of champagne?'

Remember to ask yourself the question: without going over the top, what is the best and most sensible way to dress in order to create the appropriate level of influence?

Ask questions with the right tone and emphasis

Before we start this topic, I should make it clear that, whatever my skill as a writer, or how much help I get from my copy-editors, it's incredibly difficult to adequately communicate precise examples of tone and emphasis in the written word. I can do no more than rely on broad descriptions and your own sensitive, mature and subjective interpretations to finish the job for me!

One tip, however, when looking at the examples given, is to actually say them out loud a few times in order to experiment and fully understand the points that I'm making.

Emphasis

How a question comes across will often be determined by where in the sentence the emphasis is placed. Often it is this emphasis that will convey a 'feeling' or a mood to the other person, and obviously you want that person to be in a receptive frame of mind to consider your question. So where exactly should you place the emphasis? Let's look at a few examples:

Have a look at the simple question:

? So, what can you do to help me?

Now try saying it out loud with the emphasis on different words to see how this changes the feeling and mood.

Say it with the emphasis on the word **'you'** and it sounds sarcastic:

? So, what can *you* do to help me?

Say it with the emphasis on **'can'** and it looks like you are in desperate need:

? So, what *can* you do to help me?

Try it again, this time with the emphasis on the **'me'**, and it becomes much more self-centred:

? So, what can you do to help *me*?

To make the sentence sound more personal, sincere and appealing, the emphasis should be on '**help**':

? **So, what can you do to *help* me?**

Try it again, but say the whole sentence quickly, and with the emphasis on the '**what**', and you'll sound irritated and impatient:

? **So, *what* can you do to help me?**

Of course, realistically, in our day-to-day speech, we don't stop and analyse these things – we just talk! However, once you consider for a moment the importance of emphasis, it's worth making sure that, if you are preparing to 'just ask' someone for something, you give some advance thought and practice, not only to what you will say, but also to where the emphasis should lie in your question.

Tone

The actual tone of your voice is also extremely significant. Think for a moment about speech, and how the way we talk and ask questions influences how we, and those we are asking, feel. Remember, this is not a textbook on the science of vocal qualities and articulation. My aim here is merely to make you stop and be aware of its importance, and to realize that it is an issue to consider.

With this in mind, the two main techniques I want to mention are what I call '**vocal appropriateness**' and what various experts call '**vocal mirroring**'.

We've all heard people who talk very quickly or slowly, or indeed loudly or very quietly. The first thing you need to do if you want to influence someone positively when you're asking them for something, is to be 'vocally appropriate'. In other words, you should ensure that the way you speak fits the situation. A simple example of being vocally inappropriate would be speaking very loudly in a public reference library. Ask the librarian at the top of your voice for something, and they will immediately form a negative perception of you.

The second technique is 'vocal mirroring'. At its simplest, the theory goes like this: if you sound like the person you are dealing with in terms of vocal style, they will subconsciously feel more comfortable with you, and will therefore be more likely to respond favourably to your question.

This does not mean, however, that you have to impersonate them. In practice, what you need to consciously do is *listen* to their vocal mood, style, tone, volume, speed, and so on, and simply try to fall into a similar pattern.

For example, if you meet someone for a business meeting where you are hoping to sell your goods, services, or an idea, and you discover that they are very quiet and hesitant in their speech, how will it make them feel if you come across as very loud, brash and self-confident? They'll feel uncomfortable – and possibly even pressured or intimidated. It would be much more sensitive, not to mention commercially sensible, to 'mirror' their style and adapt yours to be a bit quieter and a touch more hesitant. The other person should then feel more relaxed and your meeting may go better.

The 'ups' and 'downs' of language

With regard to tone and emphasis, there is another technique that I'd like to mention. Language has its own 'music'. In the same way that a tune is made up of higher and lower notes, so is the spoken word, with different kinds of phrases following a certain pattern:

Questions go up: Ask a question and, without even thinking about it, in most cases, your emphasis will go up at the end of the sentence. Try it: ask out loud,

'How are **you**?'

Listen carefully to almost any question, and the final word normally hits a slightly higher note. Usually you don't do this on purpose – you can't help yourself. It's almost an unconscious act.

Statements stay the same:

'The sky is blue.'

' Italy won the World Cup in 2006.'

'Paris is the capital of France.'

Take note of how you say these statements out loud. Generally the tone will remain level throughout the sentence. Again, you don't think about it – it just happens like that.

Commands go down: Tell your dog to 'Sit down!' or your child to 'Stop eating that chocolate!' Pay careful attention to how these commands sound. What happens to the tone right on the last word or syllable? It goes down. As before, this is a totally unconscious act on your behalf.

So why am I telling you all this? Well, the really interesting bit about it is that because our brains are conditioned to process an upward tone as a question, and a downward tone as a command, we can have a bit of fun by deliberately reversing them. Suppose you ask a question but, instead of going up at the end you go down, and say it with slightly more 'command' tonality. The listener will process it more as a command, and will be more likely to give you the response that you are looking for. That's the theory!

Here are a couple of example questions:

? **Any chance you might give me a discount?**

Alter the way you say this by dropping the tone of the final syllable and adding a slight emphasis to the word 'give', and it becomes more of a command.

? **Would you like to go out for coffee with me sometime?**

The natural way of saying this would be to go up at the end of the sentence as it is a question. If, however, you drop the note on the last syllable and gently change the emphasis to make it sound more like a command, your request may be processed in a different way and trigger an almost automatic 'OK!'

Practise it first, then try it!

QUESTIONS TO 'JUST ASK' YOURSELF

Questions affect your ability to get what you want, not only from other people and situations, but also from yourself. Many of life's stresses and strains can be reduced, and in some cases removed altogether, simply by 'just asking' yourself the right questions. These questions are what this section of the book is all about. Hopefully you'll find some of them useful food for thought. Just ask them!

What do you want?

Given the title of this book, an important question to ask yourself is:

? What do you want?

If I asked you now to write down the things that you really wanted, most of you would find it difficult to be precise and tangible. You might have the really important general things on your list: good health, a loving and caring family and friends, a comfortable roof over your head, personal freedom, a sense of achievement and recognition, and a secure income with the time to make the most of it, perhaps.

Whilst vitally important, these things are so universal that, even when we have them, rightly or wrongly they are often taken for granted. So, let me repeat the question: *apart* from these things:

? What do you want?

Of course, there are no 'correct' answers to this question. But, as mentioned earlier in the book, in order to help you find the answers yourself, you need to narrow down your questions in order to get more specific and tangible 'wants' to aim for.

To give you a helping hand, I'm going to give you some questions to help you move forward. Regard this as your 'wants' question checklist. Run through it once a year at least, and review it periodically. Sometimes it can be productive and fun to do it with those who are close to you. Of course, my list is not meant to be exhaustive. In addition to the questions I've listed below, I am sure you can come up with other categories of your own.

Your 'wants' question checklist

? Travel: If I could visit one place I have never been to before during the next year, where would it be?

? Things: If I could acquire one thing over the next year that I don't already have, what would it be?

? New experiences: If I could try one thing I've never done before during the next year, what would it be?

? Knowledge: If I could learn more about one subject in particular over the next year, what would it be?

? **Skills:** If I could develop one new skill over the next year, which I currently don't possess, what would it be?

? **Personal career:** If I could achieve one tangible thing over the next year in my career, which I have not achieved before, what would it be?

? **Personal friendships:** If I could develop a friendship with one person whom I already know, over the next year, who would it be?

? **Habits:** If I could get rid of one bad habit this year, what would it be?

Have you got the hang of it yet? How many more questions like these can you come up with?

If you're in a permanent relationship, asking each other this sort of thing can often turn into a great conversation and you will have two 'wants' to pursue together. And once you have answers to the questions above, you can work through each of the subject areas again, this time employing a different set of questions. For example:

? How can I do that?
? What do I need to do to make it happen?
? When can it be done?
? What are the cost implications?
? How can I raise the money?

The moment you ask these questions there is a part of you that is already accepting the things you want as a reality.

Ask 'When...?'

Without wishing to bore you with the innermost workings of the Cooper household, my wife has quite ruthlessly just interrupted my writing to come and complain to me,

'I'm so frustrated! I can't find that document! We really *must* sort this stuff out!'

What I did was take a deep breath. (I wonder whether John Grisham puts up with this same problem?) Then I agreed with her, and asked her a key question:

? **OK. When?**

We now have a plan for 'sorting the stuff out', and a day set aside in the diary to deal with other related 'things'.

Asking **'When...?'** is one of the simplest and most important, yet most ignored, questions of all. In fact, if I had to single out one question as being at the top of my 'important questions' league table, then this would be it!

Why is it so important? There are two reasons. Asking 'When...?' helps with:

◆ stress-busting; and
◆ getting things to happen.

'When...?' as a stress buster

In one fell swoop, asking this question sets you on the road to dealing with one of the greatest personal barriers to success and the maintenance of good physical and mental health. I'm referring, of course, to stress.

Have you ever experienced that feeling of 'things piling up'? Before you can finish one 'thing', other 'things' get added to the pile. In fact, does the 'things pile' ever really disappear? Some people live their entire lives feeling more and more anxious, and worrying about how they are ever going to get through it all. I'd like to show you a way you can improve matters, no matter how simplistic this may seem.

First, make a list of all your commitments. Regardless of whether they are business or personal, important or trivial, put them on the list and then **'When...?'** them! In other words, go through each one in turn, and ask yourself 'When can I do that?' (Bear in mind that, contrary to what we are often told, procrastination is not necessarily a bad thing. In fact, there is nothing wrong with putting things off, so long as you know when you *are* going to do a certain thing, and you *do* it when you reach that moment.)

Having now gone through your entire list, and given each of your 'things' the **'When...?'** treatment, you'll now have a diary full of actions to perform at set times. The trick now is to forget about them until that time comes. Then, when it does, do them!

What has happened is that you've now dealt with the stress-creating issue I mentioned earlier: 'How am I ever going to get through it all?' Well, now you know you can because there is a **'When...?'** plan in place.

I accept that there may be cynics out there who will say,

'This doesn't always work,' or 'My life is too complicated,' and so on. They are probably right some of the time but, equally, this method does work most of the time. In fact, I can almost guarantee you that using this **'When...?'** approach to dealing with your 'things' will give you an immediate and immense sense of relief.

By the way, let me ask you another question:

? **When are you going to make this 'to do' list and apply this principle?**

Try it now! If you can't do it now, then *when*? At the very least, answer that question now and put it in your diary!

At the end of each day, repeat the process. Ask yourself what else should go on the list, and then just **'When...?'** it!

Ask 'When...?' to make things happen

Life has a tendency to just happen! However, to make it happen in the way we want, we need to apply the **'When...?'** rule to questions we ask.

Once we have fixed a time for something, more often than not it happens. The mere act of fixing a 'when', either in your own head because you asked yourself this question, or because you have arranged the 'when' with someone else, triggers and commands real action.

Let's take a look at a range of situations, with me asking you a few questions, so you can see how this really works:

Have you ever bumped into someone you haven't seen for a while and said,

'We must get together properly sometime'?

Just Ask

In future, don't just say this and leave it, but **'When...?'** it. If you are sincere about meeting that person again, respond with,

❓ 'You're right! *When* would be a good time for you?' Then fix it!

Have you ever had a conversation with someone about some possible future business, which ends with them saying,

'Sometime we should be able to do something together.'

You know what to do! **'When...?'** it. Ask them,

❓ '*When* do you have in mind?'

Is it the case that a significant chunk of your business comes from your existing clients and customers? If so, ask yourself these questions:

❓ When were you last in touch with them?
❓ Do you know when you are next going to have some contact?

If you can't answer these questions, then apply the **'When...?'** treatment. Create a plan of 'when' you are next going to be in contact with your most important customers and clients. This is particularly important in the service industries and in those sectors where personal relationships are key.

When are you next going to read this book?
'When...?' it!

When do I work best?

You're at work. Imagine for a moment that you have to produce a difficult piece of writing, give a presentation, make your follow-up calls, tackle a difficult strategic problem, or come up with something creative. Do you sometimes find it hard to get started, and, when you do, that it's almost impossible to produce anything worthwhile? We've all had moments like this. However, the opposite is also true.

Haven't you had moments when things have just flowed? Ideas have come, words have effortlessly and miraculously appeared on the computer screen, problems have been identified and inspirational solutions found.

Why is it that sometimes it all 'just flows' and other times it doesn't? Well, I'll be honest with you – I don't really know. What I do know, however, with absolute certainty, is that if you ask yourself the question:

? **When do I work best?**

then act on your answer, you will perhaps find that those 'flow' moments happen more frequently. All you need to do is to channel certain types of work into that optimum time slot you've identified. (You could also bear this in mind when employing the stress-busting **'When...? it'** technique discussed earlier.)

By the way, if the question throws up an answer such as,

'My best ideas come mid-afternoon when I am walking alone in the park with the dog',

or:

'I always manage to solve difficult business problems while reflecting on them with a notebook on a beach',

then it is a perfectly legitimate use of business or personal time to 'create' such situations.

By the way, *my* most productive slot of time is in the morning, and I always get my best (and wildest!) ideas when soaking in a very hot bath. My wife now encourages me to take showers...!

Where shall I keep things?

How much time do you spend a week looking for things? How often have you muttered to yourself, 'Where is that file/document/birth certificate/ password/passport/key/photograph/report/address/phone   charger/ bottle of tablets/bill/invoice/cheque/presentation/folder/diary/scrap of paper with a telephone number on it/interesting newspaper cutting/ new fountain pen that was a present from your mother-in-law/valentine card you just bought/useless thing you kept in case it "came in useful"/ object you put somewhere safe so you would know where it was when you needed it...?'

Do you have piles of 'things' on and around your desk at your office or at home? Do you have drawers and cupboards heaving with 'stuff'?

How often have you been frustrated at the amount of time spent hunting for these 'precious things', or got angry with yourself and humiliated at your own uselessness for not having got it all sorted?

Most important of all – how many of these objects actually have a proper designated place in your office or home, or a system to enable them to be found quickly? Have you even asked yourself that question? Ask it now:

? **Where should I/we keep X?**

I'm not concerned with your answer. What's important to me is that you ask this question. Once you've asked it, come up with a simple system in response to it, and you will slowly begin to reduce some of that 'hunting time'.

Remember, you don't have to deal with everything in one go! At home, my wife and I asked this question just in relation to all our various keys that were dotted around the house. I'm not telling you what we did with them, but we came up with an answer and sorted out the key problem.

It only took 30 years!

What am I waiting for?

Have you ever attended an interview, an audition, or put in a business proposal, only to be told, 'We'll get back to you'? How does it feel, day after day, as you scan your post and emails, or wait for the phone to ring? Well, ask yourself why you don't put yourself out of your misery and ask, 'What am I waiting for?'

What benefit do you gain by waiting and waiting to hear? One thing is for sure – if they liked you and what you had to offer, they won't reject you simply because you contacted them (within a sensitive time frame) and asked politely whether they had any feedback for you yet.

There is only a limited number of outcomes, so you have nothing to lose, really. You might get a 'yes' to whatever it is you were waiting to hear about, so that's 'good news'. But if you get a 'no', then at least you can get on with your life without further anxiety and make future plans. The other possibility is that you might be told, 'We are still in the middle of the decision-making process.' If this is the case, then at least you have reminded them about you and have shown that you are interested and committed.

The real reason people simply sit and wait is out of fear that they will get the answer they don't want to hear!

Get rid of your 'waiting anxiety' and ask for feedback!

Can I do both, neither, or something completely different?

Here's a strange fact of human behaviour: ask someone to choose between two options and the majority of people will do just that. Notwithstanding the fact that there might be more than two options, or that neither of those offered are acceptable, most people feel almost compelled to select from the two on offer.

As you've already seen elsewhere in the book (page 77), there are powerful ways you can use this to influence others to your advantage. Most importantly, however, be careful not to fall into the trap yourself.

Let me give you a business example:

I was consulted by a client over the telephone for advice on when to launch a new product. After some discussion about the material and the marketing objectives, the simple question I was asked was, 'Should we seek media coverage for this before or after a specific event was going to happen?'

For half an hour we batted the pros and cons backwards and forwards like a couple of tennis players.

'Just a moment,' I said. 'Have you asked yourself whether you could do both or neither?'

The moment I said it, I could sense the relief. My caller realized they were trapped by their own self-imposed question and choices.

In practice, I showed how doing both could be beneficial, but I also questioned the wisdom of their particular strategy as a whole. This led to discussions about alternatives. They have now decided to develop their service in a totally different way and, at the time of writing, are on the verge of a major commercial breakthrough.

The key question here is:

? **Can I do both, neither, or something completely different?**

Strangely enough, the answer is almost always 'yes'!

Do I *really* know what I'm talking about?

How often have you found yourself talking about something you really don't know about? I mean putting forward views, advice and opinions on a topic of which you have no prior experience or in which you have no formal training? Well, it actually happens all the time – in business, professional and personal situations.

In business you make financial decisions and marketing plans based on what? Your years of experience and training in these areas? Almost daily I have conversations with business or professional people who tell me, usually on a one-to-one basis in an embarrassed whisper,

'I'm not a marketing person!'

In the next breath they are telling me what marketing decisions they have taken, and how they want me to execute their plan for them.

Or I listen to people chatting to me about their pension plans and investment strategies as though they were personal financial planning experts.

How many times have you been on the receiving end of medical advice, DIY tips, gardening advice, or personal relationship guidance from people who have no more expertise in these matters than you do?

Next time you are tempted to give such advice, just ask yourself:

? **Do I really know what I'm talking about?**

If not, keep quiet!

Do my advisers *really* know what they are talking about?

Perhaps even more dangerous is getting advice – even professional advice – from so-called 'experts', who themselves don't know what they are talking about. Yet it happens all the time. Not necessarily through dishonesty, but simply because the advisers have not asked themselves the question mentioned on the previous page: 'Do I really know what I'm talking about?' There's an old saying: a little knowledge is a dangerous thing.

If you give professional advice, here are a couple of difficult questions to ask yourself:

? **How often do I say, 'I don't know'?**
? **Am I specialized enough?**

In fact, do you actually know what you don't know?

Often, a particular issue or question requires a specialist – not someone with a general knowledge of the area. Often, that specialist will identify things from long experience and gut instinct that a general adviser might miss. If you are getting advice, get help from the most experienced specialist you can find.

The key question you should be asking an adviser before taking them on is:

? **How often have you encountered this situation before and helped get the desired result?**

The decision-makers in a major, market-leading organization decided for themselves that a television advertising campaign was the way forward. They asked me to sit in on the presentations they were getting from some advertising agencies, and to be their 'bullshit detector' (their phrase, not mine!). They were smart enough to know that, not having been through this before, they might miss the 'bullshit'.

I spent a very amusing day watching these presentations and adding my views here and there, which, in the main, were disregarded. Eventually they appointed an agency to advise on and produce a television advert for them, investing thousands of pounds in the project. This was an agency who had some good ideas and who had got good results in the past, but who had never worked in the same, very specialist, niche sector as the organization in question. Thus the 'bullshit' only started after the appointment of the agency was made.

Only after the advert was produced did they then ask my opinion as the specialist in this particular sector. Diplomatically I told them why I didn't think it would get the results they hoped for and deserved. Not surprisingly, they justified the material and continued. They even had a special phone system installed to cope with all the enquiries.

The results? Very disappointing!

The organization had essentially failed to get the results they wanted for one main reason. They didn't ask themselves:

?   **Do your advisers really know what they are talking about?**

Could I be wrong?

Have you ever come home from work angry at something your boss has said, or because of a difference of opinion with a work colleague? How often have you argued with your spouse or partner over something? Isn't it the case that the more you think about the situation, talk about it and 'mentally replay' the moment of injustice, the more uptight you feel about it?

Well here's a simple but important question to ask yourself:

? **Could I be wrong?**

Think back. Aren't there times in your past when you have been in the wrong? So ask yourself – is this another one of those times?

If this question is a bit too much for you, try a different one that will have a similar effect:

? **If I were standing in the other person's shoes, could I see why they would think I was in the wrong?**

If the answer is 'yes', then you are on the road to making peace both with yourself and with the other person.

Who should do what?

If you're ever involved in some activity involving another person, or a group of people, one of your first questions ought to be, '**Who should do what?**'

One of the most common causes of lack of success and potential arguments is that nobody has consciously asked this incredibly basic and common-sense question out loud for discussion and agreement. All too often people just get stuck into whatever needs doing.

The question simply recognizes that some people are naturally better at certain tasks than others. Identify who is good at what and make sure that this is reflected in whatever needs to be done.

Here's a simple, personal example:

On long journeys, my wife and I used to take turns to navigate and drive. After all, spreading the load seemed only fair. The results, however, were usually a recipe for argument. With my navigation we would end up taking the longest possible route, getting hopelessly lost and arguing a lot. My wife would get incredibly stressed at having to drive, and I would get horribly uptight at having to sit helplessly in the passenger seat watching her.

The moment we stopped trying to be fair and democratic, and asked ourselves the simple question, 'Who should do what?', things got much better. I now do most of the driving and she does all the navigating. Now we hardly ever get lost and neither of us gets too stressed over the 'driving'!

Remember, the key question, no matter what your activity, is to 'just ask':

? **Who should do what?**

What do I have to be grateful for?

Too many of us spend a disproportionate amount of time feeling depressed and down about what we don't have, or about our apparent lack of direction or success. Our focus, all too often, is on getting 'more', and on achieving that seemingly elusive 'happiness' we all strive for.

Whilst it's natural to desire progress and positive change, and this entire book is based on the notion of simply 'asking' for what you want, occasionally it is very therapeutic to 'just ask' yourself the following very simple question:

? **What do I already have to be grateful for?**

Don't just think this question – ask it out loud when you are on your own, and actually either verbalize your answers or, even better, write them down. Believe it or not, this is a very simple and powerful exercise. It almost always makes you feel better. If you want to create even more personal leverage, immediately before asking yourself this question, sit down and watch the national and international television news on any night.

After its daily dose of world disaster, war, accidents and murders, your personal list of the things you have to be grateful for will seem incredibly positive. Perspective is important!

Who are my top ten most admired people?

Some years ago, over a business breakfast meeting, a client and business colleague I had been dealing with for several years told me I was on his 'top ten list of most admired people'. Not surprisingly, I was extremely flattered. It also got me thinking. I realized that I liked the notion of having a top ten list of people who were most admired.

? Who's on your top ten list?

Try to answer this question either out loud or on paper. They don't have to be the 'great and good', the 'rich and famous', or the most educated or intelligent. On your list might be your next-door neighbour, a member of your family or personal social contacts.

As you put this list together, ask yourself what it is about those people that you particularly admire. It might be their sense of fun, their organizational skills, or even their ability to deal with horribly difficult times with a smile on their face.

Finally, ask yourself what personal strategies you could adopt in order to model the qualities and attributes of the people you admire most.

Give it a go – it can be a very powerful exercise!

When am I next in touch?

Whenever you've had a successful meeting with a business contact, or a positive outcome with a client or customer, or even just an enjoyable get-together with a friend for social purposes, ask yourself this important question:

? **When am I next in touch with them?**

If you don't have the answer, then you should have!

Why is this so important? Well, if you look at it from a business perspective, in many sectors, up to 80% of revenue is generated by returning clients and customers' word-of-mouth recommendations, or by third-party professional introductions from people you know.

So, as a piece of business or job is completed, ask yourself when you'll next be in touch with them. In your own mind, create a timescale and a reason, and put it in your diary or contact system. By keeping in touch you foster customer and client ownership and the likelihood of more successful business with them.

From a personal and social point of view, isn't it the case that there are people with whom you have simply just lost touch, not necessarily because you've fallen out with them, but because 'life' has caused you to drift apart? Isn't it also true that the longer the time has been since you last had any contact, the harder it seems to be to get back in touch with them again?

With these thoughts in mind, then, for a healthy social life and your future business prosperity, always ask yourself the all-important question, **'When am I next in touch?'**

If I had an extra day off each week, what would I do with it?

Many people, if asked, say they would love to have more free time. Yet, those same people, when suddenly faced with the time they have craved, simply don't know what to do with it!

If this is you, then ask yourself right now:

? If I had an extra day each week, what would I do with it?

'The answers are all out there, we just need to ask the right question.'

Oscar Wilde, Irish dramatist and poet

(1854–1900)

? 135

Just Ask

What would I most like to change about myself?

This is a potentially painful question, and one to ask in a moment of reflection and solitude.

❓ **What three things would you most like to change about yourself?**

Take your time and write them down.

Then play the 'time travellers' game'. Imagine you could travel one year into the future and observe yourself without these changes being made.

❓ **What would you be like?**
❓ **How would you look?**
❓ **What would the consequences be for yourself and those around you?**
❓ **What would be the worst possible scenario if you didn't act now and didn't make any changes?**

Now fast-forward your imaginary 'time machine' and take a look at yourself from the perspective of three, five and ten years into the future.

❓ **How do you physically look then?**
❓ **What might have happened to you and the people close to you by then if you have not started to make changes?**

I can tell you – you won't always like what you see! If you don't, then once you're back in the present, ask yourself what practical steps and actions you need to take to make the necessary changes.

❓ **Who can help you to make the changes?**

The emotional leverage created by your imaginary visit into the future ought to compel you to take the actions you've been putting off!

Can I say 'no'?

Have you ever taken on too much, either at work or in your personal life? Have you ever found yourself committing yourself to doing things or being involved in something that you don't really want to do? There are a number of reasons that contribute to personal and business stress and anxieties, and saying 'yes' too often is one of them.

With this in mind, there's a very simple question you should ask yourself when you're asked to do something:

? **Can I say 'no'?**

Many people say 'yes' because it seems easier than saying 'no', and they simply don't have an immediate and plausible excuse. Sometimes, particularly in business, it's tough to turn work down for fear that you might not get asked again. In a personal situation, you might feel obligated to the person who is asking you to do something.

In most cases, however, actually you *can* say 'no'. The only real issue for you is how to do it For those of you who fall into this trap, try this sort of question response with your own variations to suit the circumstances:

? **Do you know what? I'm really flattered to be asked, and my instinct is to say 'yes', but saying 'yes' all the time is beginning to be a real problem for me. I'm trying very hard at the moment to learn how to say 'no' to things because of the amount I have on. So if I decline this time around with apologies, can you understand why this is the case?**

Of course, you don't have to treat this as a script. The gist of it, however, is very simple. You're getting the other person to process your dilemma with a question, which puts them in a position where they find it difficult to do anything other than align with your situation. Why? Because, in many cases, they will recognize it in themselves and respect you for your ability to decline in such an elegantly simple way.

What are the 'riches beneath my castle'?

Often we're so busy trying to create new opportunities for ourselves, either in business or our personal lives, that we ignore the ones we already have. When I'm wearing my 'business development hat', clients often ask me,

'What's the best way to market ourselves in order to win more business?'

My answer often shocks them. I frequently explain to them that even if they market themselves well, it's unlikely to win them new business. The most it will do is to create inquiries and opportunities for them that they then need to convert. I then usually turn the tables on them with a question. If you are in business, let me ask you a few key questions now and eventually you'll see what I'm getting at:

? How many new enquiries for business do you get each day, either by phone or face to face?

? What are the percentage success rates of the various people who deal with these inquiries?

What I'm really getting at in this example is this: the inquiries that you already have may be the 'riches beneath your castle'. It may be that you don't need to create more inquiries, because you have sufficient already. It's possible, however, that the real problem is your lack of ability to convert the calls you do get into profitable business.

I once worked with a particular organization who, with my help, identified the fact that they got three new 'cold' inquiries per day, worth an average minimum of £700 per job if they got it. Over 50 working weeks this was 750 calls in the year, worth a potential revenue to them of £525,000.

Before they spent a penny on future marketing, I got them to do these calculations and tell me what their current conversion rates were from their existing inquiries. They told me they converted 20% of the calls they got into business. Over a period of two days, I showed them how they could use conversational question techniques to get their conversion rate up. After a month they wrote and told me it had risen to 48%, and after three months they were converting 75% of their leads into business. One final point to make in this example – they also increased their prices!

The moral of this tale is simple. By examining what they already had, and by giving more attention to this, they were able to get the outcome they really wanted.

This principle may also work in your personal life. For example:

? How many existing friends do you have, with whom you just need to nurture your relationship a little more in order to make it grow?

? How many useful things have you relegated to the loft that you could put to good use?

? How many good ideas for things have you had in the past that you could exploit now?

? What skills do you have that you use in one area, which could be adapted for use in others?

Ask yourself what are the 'riches beneath your castle', and what can you do with them?

How important is it really?

Do you know what? Many of us spend a massive amount of our time getting upset over 'things', arguing with people, or struggling inside with emotional turmoil over a whole range of issues. Did something upset you last week? What about the week before? Can you even remember what it was?

When you find yourself getting churned up over something that has happened, or because of something somebody has said, ask yourself this simple question:

?   How important is it?

Is it something that's going to be of any real consequence in a year, month or even tomorrow? If the answer is 'no', sometimes it's simply best to let it go.

This doesn't mean that you have to allow yourself and your feelings to be trampled all over, but this question ought to help you keep things in perspective. Sometimes the emotional aggravation of arguing, trying to prove your point or 'teaching the other person a lesson' is disproportionate to the issue itself.

So, don't forget, when you feel yourself getting uptight, ask yourself how important it really is!

Can I have New Year today?

What do we do on New Year's Day? No, I'm not talking about taking the hangover pills! Many of us make New Year's resolutions. Just because the old year has gone, we feel we can begin again with a new and fresh start. For example, we resolve to stop biting our nails, to be more organized at home, to get fit and lose weight, and so on.

However, there's an important question to ask whenever we focus on things we would like to change about our own behaviour and attitude, and this is it:

? **Can we have New Year today?**

In other words, do we *have* to wait for the first day of January each year before we're allowed to be serious about making some personal changes? For once I do know the answer to this question. No, we don't!

For the purposes of making a fresh start, you can pretend it's New Year whenever you want, and you're not limited by your own past lack of success. If you've tried before, 'just ask' yourself these questions:

? **Why didn't it work last time?**
? **What can I do differently this time?**

Happy New Year!

Am I guilty of
'paralysis by analysis'?

Do you ever spend time agonizing so much over things that they never get done at all? Do you ever miss out on good opportunities because you are striving for the perfect answer?

> I had a client many years ago who decided that, for the first time ever, they needed a glossy brochure to promote their various services. I had been asked to guide and help them with this process. Guess how long it took from the day the first word was drafted to them holding the brochure in their hands? Six weeks? Three months? Try again! It took them over *four years*!
>
> This was because they over-analyzed every word and choice as if their lives depended on it. It culminated with a three-hour meeting in a beautiful boardroom, where 20 senior members of the organization argued over what percentage shade of grey would go on the front cover!
>
> In their efforts to get it right, their 'paralysis by analysis' had cost them four years of missed opportunities, during which time they didn't have the promotional material they had decided they needed.

Sometimes, you just need to stop over-thinking and simply act on your best instinct. Ask yourself whether the extra time, stress and mental exercise justifies what you lose or miss out on whilst you are doing your thinking.

Are my arrangements still OK?

Have you ever arrived at a business meeting only to find that the address or time you had been given had been changed, or that the person you were supposed to meet wasn't able to make it? Have you ever walked up to the reception desk at a hotel to discover the room you had booked several weeks or months earlier had been given to someone else?

It almost happened to me very recently:

> I had been engaged to do some presentation skills training for a company several months in advance. They told me when they booked me that they would arrange for me to stay in a particular hotel, and gave me the details. Being a trusting soul I accepted this. A week before the session, however, a cynical and nagging little voice in my head told me to check with the hotel.

> Guess what? They had no record of any booking for me, and were now full anyway. Not surprisingly, I got back to my client and told them this. No problem, they said. They would sort it out. Two days later I got an email confirming I had been booked into a different hotel. I couldn't resist checking with the hotel. Again they had no room booked for me! They did have a record of it being booked by my client but, as they had not received the written confirmation they had requested, they had cancelled it. They, too, were now full. This time I did what I normally do. I sorted it out myself and found a different hotel.

Now, I'm not suggesting these sorts of experiences are everyday occurrences, but we all know they do happen, and usually in circumstances where they cause maximum inconvenience. There's a simple solution to avoid this problem. Ask the person or organization you've made arrangements with to confirm everything is still on, and that your understanding of the details is correct.

So, if you want peace of mind, and to minimize any practical problems if things have changed without you knowing about it, ask a cynical question to check the arrangements.

Ask the simple question first

Have you ever been embarrassed by the fact that you've missed the obvious? Have you ever sought complex responses and solutions when the answer is right there staring you in the face?

> Whilst writing this book I got frustrated one day when my printer stopped printing properly. No subtle warnings like semi-legible faded ink marks on my paper. No – all I got out of my machine were perfectly empty white sheets. I knew it couldn't possibly be the ink cartridge because it had been replaced two days earlier, and anyway it had been used only ten minutes before it threw in its blank towel! I fiddled with its connectors, opened the printer program on my computer, got out the technical handbook, read my warranty, prepared to do battle with the technical helpdesk, and got irritable.
>
> One of my sons witnessed this shocking display of temperament and embarrassed me by asking me,
>
> 'Have you tried a different ink cartridge? Perhaps the one that you bought is faulty?'
>
> 'No, it can't be that,' I said, as my patience waned even more. 'You see, the thing is that...' (I began to rant again.)
>
> By this time my smug teenage son had fitted and tested a new cartridge, which worked perfectly. He just smiled and said,
>
> 'Dad. Always remember to ask a simple question first!'

I dedicate this piece of advice to him.

LIFE SITUATIONS: THE QUESTIONS TO 'JUST ASK...'

Well, I've identified the golden rules of asking, given you pages of 'Just Ask' techniques to adapt and try out, and suggested a number of questions you can ask yourself in order to influence your own thinking and actions.

In this final section, the aim is to take a look at how some of the issues we have looked at throughout the book can be put into practice in certain basic, everyday situations where it would be helpful to have a new focus and some 'magic' questions to ask.

When making decisions

Let me begin this section by repeating something very important from the beginning of this book as a reminder:

The decisions we take in life, and the results that flow from these decisions, are influenced by the questions we ask. Therefore, the quality of those questions affects our decisions and their ultimate outcome.

Ask more and better questions, and more often you will get better results!

When it comes to decision-making, we have all experienced moments when we've been faced with really difficult choices to make. How does it feel to know that your decision will most likely have a huge impact on your future? Have you ever heard a voice in your head screaming, 'Help! I don't know what to do!'? The purpose of this part of the book is to give you a few general questions to ask yourself, which will act as a powerful stimulus to help you look at things in a way that triggers the right decision for you.

Have you ever had a 'That's it!' moment? By this I mean a moment when, having agonized over an issue you haven't been able to make a decision on, something (or someone) suddenly prompts a thought in you that makes you shout, 'Yes! That's it! Now I know what I'm going to do!' In order to prompt more of these 'That's it!' moments, or at the very least to help you to address your decisions with a clear head, I'm going to give you a list of questions to think about.

To begin with, however, I want to give you my three 'pre-decision-making' questions, which I consciously ask myself before wrestling with the issue itself. Here they are:

? 1. Am I in the right physical and mental state to make a decision?

As a basic rule, if you're not in the right state, don't attempt to make a final decision. Perhaps you might be feeling low or depressed. Maybe you're ill, or have just got some bad news. The bottom line is this: if your physical or mental state is going to affect your thinking in some way then, if you possibly can, save your decision-making until you're more 'yourself'.

? **2. Is there anyone else I can talk to who can help me with this decision?**

Whilst ultimately the final decision will be yours, it's easier if you are able to bounce your thoughts off someone else. My simple advice, then, is to ask yourself, 'Who else can I share this with?'

? **3. Do I have sufficient factual information to come to a proper decision?**

It's astonishing how many people try to make decisions based on insufficient information. Ask yourself whether there are gaps in your knowledge. What else do you need to know? Where can you get that information?

And now for those 'That's it!' moment-triggering questions!

What feels right?

One of the great causes of stress in decision-making situations is the notion that there is an absolute 'right' decision, and that if you talk, think, debate and beat yourself up long and hard enough you will eventually arrive at an answer that leaves no room for doubt.

However, decision-making is not an exact science. Sometimes you have to proceed with confidence one way or the other based on what *feels* right. If this is a bit too vague for you, try a different question. Ask it out loud, and answer according to your gut-instinct feel and conscience, regardless of whether your response seems logical or not. The question is:

? **Which route instinctively gives me the most peace of mind?**

Learn to listen to this inner answer.

Some years ago I had a difficult personal business decision to make. The deal that I had been offered seemed to be a good one in all respects, yet for some reason or other there was a niggling little voice in my head saying 'Don't do it!' In fact, I decided to go ahead and do it anyway. Why not? After all, from a cold, logical, business point of view, the deal made sense. Yet, within a year it was obvious I had got it wrong.

It was an expensive lesson to learn. From then on, whatever you want to call it – sixth sense, divine intervention, self-doubt, common sense – I have listened very carefully to that mysterious voice of reason in my head and acted upon it.

What if I make the wrong decision?

Sometimes I've been in situations where people have asked my advice because they were not sure what to do. When I've suggested one course of action, they've responded with,

'Yes, but what if such-and-such a thing were to happen?'

'OK then,' I reply. 'What about the other option?'

The answer I have regularly received is,

'Well, I can't do that either because what if...?'

Now they have ruled out both choices by playing the 'What if...?' game.

When you get to this sort of 'thought block', try these questions to clear your thinking. If you *were* to get it wrong:

? What would be the worst consequences of getting it wrong?
? Could you live with these consequences?
? At that time, could you change your mind or revert to an acceptable alternative?

If you knew that, even if it went wrong, there was a decent alternative, or if not you could still live with whatever the consequences would be, then you might have the courage to go along with your instinct instead of fearing your own personal 'What ifs?'

Along with these questions you could also ask,

? What if I were right?
? What's the very best that could happen?

Now ask yourself whether the potential benefits of your decision, if it's the right one, outweigh the possible negative consequences of getting it wrong?

If people are involved, do I have doubts about them?

There will be occasions when your decision really comes down to the people that you might be dealing with if you choose a particular course of action. Someone may have made you a business proposal that seemed fantastic, or, on a personal level, maybe someone has invited you to do something with them and you have to decide whether or not to do it.

Ask yourself these questions, and answer honestly with either a 'yes,' 'no,' or 'I have doubts' response:

? **Am I going to be able to get on with this person in the future?**
? **Do we have shared values?**
? **Do I feel comfortable around this person?**
? **Do I respect this person?**

If you have answered 'yes' to all four of these, then don't hesitate to say 'yes' to the offer or invitation (if the practical details are attractive!) If you've answered 'no' or 'I have doubts' to any of them, perhaps this will trigger a 'That's it!' moment for you, and you'll turn the deal down or decline the invitation.

If you're deciding between two options ask, 'What else could I do?'

All too often people find themselves in situations where they are so focused on deciding between two options that they forget to ask whether there are any others they could choose. In fact, sometimes the reason why making a decision is proving so difficult is because neither option is quite right.

I've often been in business situations when a client has asked my advice about whether they should do one thing or another, and I have asked them:

? **I can see why you've been debating this because, actually, I'm not sure either answer is right for you. Have you considered doing something else, which might help you achieve your objective?**

You should see the reaction, indeed the relief on their faces when I ask this! Sometimes I even get a verbal 'Yes! That's it!' response.

What is my decision-making 'track record'?

Given that in most difficult circumstances there isn't a definite right or wrong, most of us mere mortals make decisions hoping that we get them right more often than we get them wrong. With this in mind, analyze your decision-making track record. Identify the last ten really important decisions you've had to make. Go back over the years if you have to, and take your time, briefly writing them down. You might have had to decide, for example:

? Should I do that course or not?
? Which of these two new products should we launch first?
? Shall we have another child?
? Shall we increase our fees or not?
? Shall we move to another city?
? Which of those two new offices shall we rent?
? Should we buy a second home as an investment?
? Shall I accept that job, or stay where I am?
? Shall I go it alone and start my own business?

Having written down these situations, ask yourself:

? What is my track record for making the right decision?

If you have a high success rate, then you ought to be able to trust your decision-making judgement with confidence and maximum peace of mind. If, however, you've got them wrong with great regularity, then perhaps you need to take this into account when you shout 'That's it!' next time around.

Ask questions in response to the *Serenity Prayer*

Have you heard what is known as the *Serenity Prayer?* Let me share it with you:

God, grant me the serenity to accept the things I cannot change, the courage to change the things I can, and the wisdom to know the difference.

Sometimes, the subject of your decision-making may relate to issues such as:

? Shall I get involved in that situation or not?
? Shall I speak up or keep quiet?
? Do I carry on with or give up on something?

To help you create a 'That's it!' moment, use the sentiments expressed in this prayer as the basis for questions to help you make decisions in such situations. So ask:

? If I were to get involved, is this something that I could change?
? If it is something I could change or influence, do I have the courage to get involved?
? Am I wise enough to know the difference?

Answer these questions and at some point during the thought process you may well come up with your decision.

'The uncreative mind can spot wrong answers, but it takes a very creative mind to spot wrong questions.'
Anthony Jay, British writer and journalist
(1930–   )

In medical situations

Sadly, it's almost inevitable that there will be times in your life when you will have to face up to various medical problems concerning either you or close members of your family. In such situations, knowing the right questions to ask, and having the courage and techniques to ask them, could literally be a matter of life or death.

Do you find yourself tongue-tied and stressed in the presence of doctors, consultants and other medical specialists? Have you ever felt intimidated by the frantic, highly organized chaos of hospitals? Does it frustrate you that hospitals and medical institutions often seem to operate in some kind of 'time warp' where, 'I'll be back to you with those painkillers in a couple of minutes,' can often mean a wait of several hours? The truth is, when dealing with the medical world, many people find themselves sucked into an institutionalized 'maze', in which they simply feel out of control.

If any of these sorts of situations seems familiar to you, then there are two words that can make a huge difference when it comes to getting what you want in medical circumstances:

Just ask!

Seems fairly obvious, doesn't it? Perhaps, but it doesn't always happen. There are four main reasons why people don't ask enough questions to get what they want in medical situations:

◆ they haven't thought of asking;
◆ they don't know they can ask;
◆ they are afraid of asking because they are either intimidated or think they will look stupid and that it will turn them into a nuisance;
◆ they are fearful to ask in case they don't like the answer.

In this part of the book I'm going to give you several questions you can ask yourself to direct your thinking, as well as questions you can ask others in the medical world. These questions are not intended to be exhaustive – they can't possibly cover the myriad human situations that you might find yourself in. They are simply examples to stimulate the right thoughts and to empower you to 'just ask'. (Yes, I've said it again! Sorry about the repetition, but it might just save your life.)

Here, then, are some questions to consider asking *yourself*:

Should I seek a second opinion?

When should you consider asking for a second opinion? The answer to this is simple. When you don't like the first one! If the medic you have seen gives you an outcome you don't approve of, or you lack confidence in the person you have been dealing with, for whatever reason, then you should consider asking for a second opinion.

Obviously, whether or not you do this depends on the practicalities of the situation and the seriousness of the circumstances. You will have to balance your desire to see someone else with some basic common sense.

If you do want to seek another view – the politically correct phrase at present is 'further opinion' – it's worth knowing that the medical world is under instructions and guidance at the moment to 'respect' a patient's request. Ask your GP for another referral without being too personally critical of the consultant you have seen. A question like this should do the trick:

> ? I don't want to be labelled as a difficult patient, but I have gone through a list of questions with my consultant, Mr Smith, and his answers didn't really give me the peace of mind I was hoping for. Who else have you come across that I can consider seeing for a further opinion?

When was the last time I reviewed my medication?

At a dinner I attended recently, social conversation turned to who was taking the most pills. One guest boasted that he took 19 pills a day, while another competitive diner countered with, 'Well I take 11, but I also have to inject three times a day with insulin!' Don't I get to exciting social events?

The fact is, many people do take an increasingly large cocktail of medications. With this in mind, ask yourself when was the last time you asked for them to be reviewed? All you have to do is make an appointment with your GP; or nowadays many pharmacists can advise you. The sorts of questions you should be asking include:

> ? Why am I taking each pill?
> ? Do I still need to take them?
> ? Is the dosage still appropriate?
> ? Might some other treatment, or nothing at all, be better?
> ? What about the side effects?

What new research is out there that my doctors and I are not aware of?

Unfortunately, there are times when the doctors will simply say, 'There is no cure. There is nothing we can do to help.' In keeping with the spirit of the rest of this book, I strongly believe that, while there are still questions you can 'just ask', you shouldn't give up! In my opinion, this is one of those questions.

Your doctors are only human. They can only read so much, and some will be more vigilant than others when it comes to keeping up to date with new developments. Ask them politely:

? Where can I find out about new research in this area?
? Who can I talk to that specializes in this field?
? Who are the leading researchers and specialists in the world in this problem?

Alternatively, at the very least, do your own research on the internet and be prepared to follow up any names and contacts you see with questions. If you doubt the potential of this, watch the moving 1992 film *Lorenzo's Oil* about a boy who develops a disease so rare that nobody is working on a cure, so his father decides to learn all about it and tackle the problem himself.

One final question to ask yourself if you are hesitating:

? What do I have to lose?

What alternative therapies could I try?

This is similar to the question above. There are many alternative health therapists out there you might consider. Ask around to find out about them. Contact them directly and ask them:

? What exactly they do?
? What are their qualifications?
? What sort of training have they had?
? Do they belong to a professional body?
? What sort of track record of success have they had with your problem?
? Do they think they can help you with your problem?

Who can I talk to for help and support?

You don't always have to deal with your problems alone. Out there you will find an association, a society, a charity, a local support group or even a kind individual who can help, because more often than not they will have faced a similar problem.

How do you find such support? Get in touch with your doctors, friends, contacts or local libraries, or search the internet, and 'just ask'!

Where else can I get treatment?

If you can't get treatment in your own city or country within an acceptable time frame, at least ask yourself (and those you are dealing with) if there are any alternatives.

In most cases it's only by asking that you might find out about other possibilities. For example, did you know that the UK has reciprocal healthcare arrangements with some other countries and territories, which means you are entitled to urgent treatment either at reduced cost or free?

If you did know, check it out. If you didn't, isn't it amazing what you can discover if you 'just ask'.

What's going on?

Have you ever been in hospital as a patient, or with a close family member, where the real problem has been one of communication? No matter what you do, you just can't seem to find out exactly what's going on with your case. Junior doctors will tell you,

'It's up to the consultant to decide what the treatment should be, and whether or not to operate.'

'When will he be around to talk to then?' you ask, only to get the reply, preceded by a sharp intake of breath,

'Impossible to tell, really. It could be any time – he's very busy.'

Does this sound familiar? Without wanting to get too political, I have personal experience of patients going for days without being able to get the information they want, and having to live with the anxiety and practical difficulties that this situation creates.

Here is what you do. You need to ask a **'how'** or **'when'** question of the right person. Whilst I can't give you a technique that will work with every consultant in every hospital in the country, from practical experience and trial and error I have had considerable success with this.

Most consultants have a secretary or personal assistant. Make it your business to find out who he or she is, along with their telephone number and email. The senior nursing staff on the ward will usually give you this information if you ask, or a call to the hospital's central switchboard will normally produce results. Armed with this number I have, in the past, rung it and said something along the lines of:

'My name is Ian Cooper, my son is a patient of Mr Shrub. I apologize for contacting you directly, but I wonder if you can help? We have a few questions and concerns about my son's condition and proposed treatment, but we haven't yet managed to speak to Mr Shrub directly. It would be really helpful if you could let me know when would be a good time today, either to get him on the phone for a few minutes or to arrange to see him personally?'

On the occasions I have done this, I have either been put through to the consultant immediately, if he has been available, or I have been given a time slot to see him. At the very least my question and direct approach have usually brought me closer to getting the information I want.

Questions to ask if you are told you need some sort of treatment, operation or medical procedure

Take this list with you, or even the book, for confidence! Tell the consultant, specialist or doctor right at the beginning:

> ? I hope you don't mind but I've prepared a whole list of questions I need to ask you. So will you please make sure you leave time for me to go through them before we finish?

As you ask this, physically get your list out and put it in front of you. It makes it harder to ignore.

Some suggested questions as a general starting point:

> ? Why exactly do you think this course of action is essential?
> ? If you didn't do this, what else might help?
> ? What is the best possible outcome I can hope for?

 158

? What are the risks?
? Who exactly will carry out the procedure?
? How many times has this person carried out this procedure and with what success rate?
? What if I choose not to have it done?
? If it were you or a member of your family with this problem, what would you do?
? Are there any other questions you think I have missed?
? If I were to want a further opinion, just for peace of mind, how would I go about getting hold of my X-rays and test results?

I hope you remain healthy enough to make this the least-read section in the book.

'Every clarification breeds new questions.'

Arthur Bloch, US author

When making deals

Whether you are moving home and buying and selling houses; carrying out complex negotiations on a business transaction at work; sorting out who is going to do what at your annual cricket club social fundraiser; or bidding for Mayfair over a game of Monopoly, you will no doubt have found yourself in a deal-making situation at some time or another. More importantly, however, I can guarantee that you will also have to make deals with people in the future.

In this part of the book, I want to show you that the key to making good deals is 'just asking' good questions. Before I go any further, it's important to bear in mind that this is not a book on negotiation skills. However, I do want to give you a few general questions to 'just ask' yourself, or whoever you are seeking to make a deal with, which should help you to maximize your chances of getting what you want.

First of all, here are a few simple, general rules and questions that often get forgotten in the cut and thrust of 'making the deal'. Try to remember to actively apply them:

Who goes first?

Before you dive in with your proposal, suggestion or price 'just ask' yourself:

> **?** Would it be better for you to go first, or to let the other person open?

Whilst of course there are always exceptions, my advice is, wherever possible, to do your best to get the other party to go first. This gives you maximum flexibility to either accept, suggest an alternative or walk away altogether. By getting them to show their cards first you retain the position of greatest control.

Of course, it may not always be easy to make this happen, but you should at least try. Remember my rule from earlier in the book:

He or she who asks the questions controls the conversation.

If you're selling your car, for example, you might be asked,

'How much do you want for it?'

Instead of answering, you should seek to respond with a control-taking question:

? **Well, how much would you be prepared to pay?**

You'll be surprised how often such a response will get an opening offer because most people find a direct question almost impossible to ignore.

If I were in their shoes, how would it feel?

This is an important one. By asking this question you force your mind to respect the fact that the other person will want to feel good about the eventual deal too. Your aim is not to get what you want at their expense, but to find a mutually beneficial solution or level that works for you both. So ask yourself these sorts of questions:

? **How important is this negotiation for them?**
? **What are their possible options and responses likely to be?**
? **What are the benefits for them of your specific proposal?**
? **What is the deal that they will be hoping to do?**
? **What will make them feel good about the final outcome?**
? **What common interests or principles do they have which you can align with?**
? **What reasons might they have for turning you down?**
? **What questions might they want to 'just ask' you?**

Once you have seen the world through their eyes you're in a much stronger position to negotiate.

Don't be a mind-reader. Ask blunt questions!

Instead of attempting to mind-read the other person, and guess what their position and stance might be, you could actually ask them outright, albeit using some of the 'softening' techniques I've mentioned elsewhere. For example:

? **Forgive me asking a really blunt question, but what exactly are you hoping to get out of this deal with us?**
? **What do you see as the most important benefits of working with us?**

Just Ask

Once you start asking questions and getting them talking you will be astonished how much ammunition they will give you to use.

I arrived at a client's office one day to run a training course for them. Whilst I was sitting in the reception area, one of the partners asked me in for a private word. He showed me a letter from a major organization, which told my client that they were being invited to pitch for a substantial piece of business and asked them to confirm they were interested and to submit details of their fees. My client wanted to know what to put.

I told them not to put anything until we had found out more about what they were looking for. I made the call and asked blunt questions. During the call I asked them how they would ultimately make a decision, and what sort of fee structure and levels they would find attractive. Believe it or not, because I had asked, they not only told me, but also mentioned the fee levels of other firms they had already received prices from.

Armed with all this, my client was able to enter the negotiation and get the job at a level that was good for both parties.

What deal would I be happy with?

Don't 'wing it'! Sort out in your own mind, before you get involved in trying to make a deal, what you would be happy with and on what terms. That way you will know when to accept or when to walk away.

Ask feedback questions

Getting a response in a negotiation, even a negative one, is better than getting none. To make sure you get a reply of some sort in most situations 'just ask' the other party feedback questions.

For example, if you have suggested a price, ask:

? How does that sound?
? Would that be acceptable to you?
? Does that fit in with your expectations?
? You wouldn't be unhappy with that sort of deal, would you?

You could even ask for feedback by a specific date to increase the leverage on the other party. For example:

? When can you let me have some feedback, because I can only
hold that deal until Thursday?

What else might be negotiable or traded?

When it comes to business deals and even personal financial transactions,
the focus, more often than not, is on money. Try asking yourself what
other factors might become part of the negotiation. If you want to
negotiate the price downwards, you need to ask yourself:

? What else can I offer in return?

Playing 'swaps' is worth considering as a trading chip!
You could ask:

? If I were to do such-and-such for you, would you help me with
something else, without any money changing hands?

Other things to think of building into the equation might be:

Timescale:
? I'll tell you what, if I get it to you by tomorrow would you be
prepared to pay us our initial asking price?

Future promotion:
? If we were to promote your service to our client base, how much
of a discount will you offer us?

What other negotiable factors can you think of in the situations in
which you find yourself?

How can I build rapport?

There's an old saying: '**People buy people first.**' In practice, what this
means is that you are more likely to make a great deal with people you
get on with. With this in mind, before you get too far into the deal-making
discussion itself, 'just ask' yourself:

? What can I do or say to create the right environment in which to
discuss the deal?
? What can I do to get the other party into the right state to be
receptive to my proposal?
? What can I do to help them?

?   **What can I ask to get them chatting about themselves?**

Remember, too, it is not just *what* you say, but also how you say it!

Think back to the **'Technology of Questions™'** section, which talks about tone, vocal emphasis, body language and gestures. Here I explained how what you say – that is, the actual words you use – accounts for a relatively small proportion of effective communication. You might find it helpful at this stage to look back over that section again – it will give you some useful tools to help you positively influence people on a non-verbal level.

'To find the exact answer, one must first ask the exact question.'

S. Tobin Webster, US lexicographer

(1758–1843)

When making conversation

Have you noticed how some people seem to get on with everybody? Have you ever been to a business or personal social event and been impressed by people who seem to flit from person to person, making animated conversation? Are you expected to turn up at business networking events by your company to 'work the room'? Do you feel nervous or apprehensive at social gatherings, worrying about whom you will talk to and what you will say?

What is the secret of being good at conversation? Is there something that successful, seemingly relaxed conversationalists do that others don't? The answer is yes! If you want to be good at conversation, and effective in both business and personal social situations, then all you need to do is master two skills:

Learn to ask questions

Listen to the answers

It's as simple as that!

I could write about these two attributes in great detail and at great length, but the art of conversation is such a huge topic that it could amount to a book in its own right. However, given the purpose of this book and the space available, this section aims simply to highlight the biggest practical question of all – the one that gives people the most anxiety in social situations: what to talk about.

What shall I talk about?

The simple answer is to ask people about subjects that you might have in common, whilst trying to avoid 'closed' questions – that is, those that can be answered with either a simple 'yes' or 'no' (or a grunt!). Subjects might include people, places, opinions or even an experience.

If this sounds difficult, and doesn't help much, then let me simplify it by telling you that there's one thing you absolutely have in common with anyone you meet at any personal or business social event or situation. You can always use it as an opening icebreaker. Do you know what it is? It is that **you are both there!**

Just Ask

You can always initiate a conversation by asking a question that relates to you both being wherever you are. Let me give you some examples.

If you meet someone you've never set eyes on before at a private and personal social function, you could ask:

? **So, how do you know Bob?**
? **Are you on the bride or groom's side?**

If it's a business event, such as a seminar, you could ask:

? **What did you think of the speaker?**
? **Are you a regular attendee at this sort of function?**

Even random meetings with people on a train or plane give you the common ground of a shared experience to use as a question icebreaker to make initial conversation:

? **So, how long do you think the delay will be?**
? **Do you do this journey regularly?**

So now you've got the conversation going, how do you keep it going? Well, personally, I have five general topics on my 'small talk' question list. All I have to do is frame questions around them. For those of you who think some of these are a bit basic, simple and contrived you would be absolutely right – that's why it is called 'small talk'. But don't knock it! Think for a second about your closest friends, the business contacts that you get on well with, your husband, wife, boyfriend, girlfriend or partner. Think about the first time you met them. Isn't it the case that your first conversation with them was simply 'small talk'? Remember, 'small talk' can lead to 'big things'!

Here, then, are my topics:

◆ work or business;
◆ home;
◆ family;
◆ holidays;
◆ current topics.

There are some examples of good questions to ask on each of these topics below.

Work or business-based questions

Here are a few examples to get you going. By the way, note how some are business-related, while some are more focused on the individual concerned:

- **?** What do you do for a living?
- **?** So, what exactly does your company do?
- **?** How long have you been doing that?
- **?** How large is your operation?
- **?** How did you get into that area of work?

Home-based questions

These are simple non-intrusive easy-to-ask personal but practical questions which will give you a bit of insight into the individual you are talking to. They are great as 'ice breakers' and almost always spark other conversational topics. Some examples are:

- **?** What was the weather like in... ?
- **?** Where arc you from?
- **?** How did you get here today?
- **?** When are you going back?
- **?** How long have you lived there?

Family-based questions

As you get into a general conversation, this category will often give you common ground with the person you're talking to. The sort of questions you could ask are:

- **?** So, do you have children?
- **?** How many do you have?
- **?** How old are they?
- **?** What do they do?
- **?** Oh, so they're studying. Where are they? What are they doing?
- **?** So, what's it like being a grandparent?

Holiday-based questions

People love talking about forthcoming holidays, or those that they have just had. For example:

- **?** So, do you have any holiday plans for the summer?
- **?** What is your favourite holiday destination?
- **?** You look very tanned! Have you just got back from somewhere? Where did you go?
- **?** I've always fancied going there. Where do you suggest we stay?

Questions about current topics

There will always be something going on locally, internationally or even on television that you can ask about. Try to avoid pure politics or religion, however, unless it is directly relevant to the event or place you are at. Try to keep it light. The sort of things you might ask are:

? So, what do you think of England's chances in the match tonight?
? So, who do you think will win Big Brother?
? Did you see that programme on television last night about the man whose arms exploded?

Avoid the social conversational traps

Regardless of whether you are in a business environment or in some form of personal social situation, there are various conversational 'question traps' that people fall into. I raise them here bluntly just to make you aware of them, so that you can ask yourself in private whether you are guilty of falling into any of them. They are:

◆ failing to listen to the answers to your questions;
◆ failing to wait for someone to answer your question, then answering it yourself;
◆ asking questions, then jumping in to talk about yourself.

Asking a question, but not listening to the answer

Let me give you a simple example. How often have you been at a party or business networking event and asked somebody their name, only to have forgotten it thirty seconds later. Have you ever blamed this embarrassing situation on your failing memory?

I have good news for you – it isn't your memory that's flagging at all. The reason you 'forgot' their name is because you weren't actually listening to their response in the first place. What you were really doing was thinking about what *you* were going to say next!

Answering your own questions before the other person has a chance to reply

Have you ever made small talk with people by asking them questions, but found yourself answering them yourself on their behalf? You may not even have noticed that you do this. Here are a number of simple examples:

? 168

'How are you feeling?' you ask.

'Better now,' you answer for them, before they have time to answer.

'What was the weather like on holiday?' you ask.

'Nice and bright I hear,' you add.

I've even come across professional salespeople doing this:

'So how does that price sound to you?' they ask, trying to close the sale. 'If it's a bit expensive, I'm sure we could trim it a bit for you,' they add, not waiting for the potential customer's response.

Can you see what I mean? Is this you? If so, you need to become conscious of the problem. It's getting in the way of effective and influential communication, and is stopping you getting what you want out of the situation. The simple and blunt rule is this:

Ask your question.

Shut up until you get an answer.

Listen to it when it comes!

Asking questions, then jumping in to talk about yourself

Asking someone a question, only to hijack their answer and turn the focus of the conversation around to yourself is another common trap – so common, in fact, that you might not even realize you are guilty of it. When you ask someone a question that prompts an interesting answer, rather than listening to what they're saying, it's all too easy to immediately jump in and relate a story of your own connected to their general response. When you do this, however, it shows that you prefer to talk rather than listen, and are more interested in yourself than in the other person. Not a great strategy for building an ongoing conversation or any lasting rapport.

Someone I hadn't seen for a long time asked me recently at a social event,

'How is your mother?'

'Actually, she's not doing too well at the moment, I'm afraid. She has Alzheimer's, and she is...' I started to say, when I was interrupted by the person who had asked me the question.

'Oh! I know all about Alzheimer's!' he began. 'There's nothing you can tell me about that – it's just terrible! My father had it, and he...'

I was then treated to a depressing 15-minute monologue on this person's father and his illness.

Now, it wasn't that I didn't care. It was just that this wasn't the subject of the conversation at that moment. Basically, if you ask someone a question, then rather than cutting them off as soon as they answer and beginning a rant of your own, you should listen to their answer properly and then ask them another question relating to their response. In most good conversations they will finish their answer with a question to you, anyway. In the example above, had I not been interrupted, I might have finished answering the question about my mother by asking the other person, 'And how is *your* father?'

Remember, a good conversation is a bit like a game of tennis, where both parties take it in turns to whack a question at each other.

'It is better to know some of the questions than all of the answers.'
James Thurber, US author, cartoonist, humorist and satirist (1894–1961)

When making or receiving a complaint

Most of us have bought goods that have turned out to be faulty or, maybe, you've been on a 'dream' package holiday, which in reality proved a nightmare? How often have you encountered unsatisfactory service of some sort, or been unhappy at the unfair way in which a friend or colleague has treated you?

At some point in your life you will have had to complain and, guess what? At some stage in the future you will have to complain again! Even worse, if you are in business, from time to time you may also find yourself on the receiving end of complaints.

What are *you* like at making complaints? Are you effective? Do you usually get what you want? How does doing it make you feel? Many people are very timid about complaining. In fact, most dissatisfied customers – 96% according to consumer research – don't complain at all!

If you doubt that figure, think back to the last time you went to a restaurant and found the food or service poor. Did you call the manager over and complain? Did you write to them afterwards, or did you do what most people do? Did you talk bravely across the table to each other about how bad the service is, and what you ought to say, but when the waiter actually asks you, 'Is everything OK?', you say and do nothing, apart from leave a tip as you leave. Come on – confession time – is this you?

So what have complaints got to do with this book? Well, the purpose here is to highlight the fact that the most effective way to complain, or indeed deal with complaints *you* receive, is to 'just ask'. Yes, questions can also be used to 'influence' the person you are dealing with when you (or they) are in complaining mode, and may help you to resolve the situation.

Not surprisingly then, many of these questions are, in fact, practical applications of some of the techniques and ideas I've already mentioned in the book. As before, some are questions you might put to others, and some are questions you need to ask yourself (for advance-planning purposes, before your complaint leaves your mouth!).

Questions to 'just ask' yourself before making a complaint

Believe it or not, one of the main reasons people fail to get a satisfactory outcome in complaint situations is simply because they haven't asked themselves the key questions first.

Here, then, are a few that you should 'just ask' yourself:

? What do I want?

It's incredibly common for people to simply blurt out their complaint without any prior thought as to what they would like from the other party. So, before launching into the complaint, ask yourself what you *want*. Are you after an apology, or an admission that they were wrong? Do you want them to take practical steps to change things about their operation or personal style in future? Perhaps you're after a refund, repair or financial compensation?

? If it's compensation I'm after, how much do I want?

You don't necessarily need to disclose this when you make your initial complaint, but you ought to have a figure in mind, otherwise you won't know when to stop complaining!

When you're asking yourself the 'How much?' question, don't just ask it from your own perspective. Ask yourself how much is actually fair and reasonable from their position too.

? What kind of documents or proof details will they want?

There may well be circumstances when it is not unreasonable for the organization on the receiving end of your complaint to ask for receipts, proof of purchase, photographs, and so on, in order to formulate a response. So, before you contact them, ask yourself what sort of details you might be asked for.

? Who precisely should I complain to?

This is a really important question. Get it wrong and you limit your chances of a successful outcome. This, of course, links in to your answer about what you are really after. For example, there is little point complaining to the porter at Leeds station that the crisps you bought on the 7.57 from Inverness to Glasgow yesterday morning were soggy!

So, before you jump in to any complaint, 'just ask' yourself who is the best person to complain to. In practice, of course, it is the person who is in a position to give you what it is you're after. If there are several options, my advice is to start at the bottom of an organization and work up, rather than the other way around. This way you are leaving yourself with another complaints channel if your first one doesn't get you the result you hoped for.

? How should I complain?

Should you do it by telephone, in person, or in writing? Which way will give you the best chance of a positive result? Does the organization you are dealing with have a formal complaints system? Do you have to follow this? Ask yourself all these questions first.

In many circumstances, the terms and conditions of your deal will set out the complaints procedure, if there is one. If so, stick to it. If you are not sure who to complain to, or how to do this, 'just ask'!

? What technique should I use?

This book has outlined several techniques for asking effective questions – you'll find them in the **'Technology of Questions™'** section. To save you reading everything again right now, however, I'll repeat a few of my own personal favourites in order to refresh your memory. You can then browse back through the book at your leisure to see what else might work for you, or what suits your situation and personality.

Don't forget to factor into your thinking, however, that it's not just *what* you say but also *how* you say it! Tone, emphasis and body language will be important. You *could* choose to go into a shop to complain and be angry, abusive and sarcastic in tone, shouting a lot and waving your arms about menacingly. Alternatively, you could be friendly and firmly polite with your complaint. Which way do you think will get you the best result?

Question techniques to employ when making a complaint

As promised, here are a few of my personal favourite 'question techniques'.

Use 'we'

One of the most effective techniques is to include the word 'we' when asking for help, which makes the issue the other person's problem as well.

? I've just taken delivery of some mail-order suitcases from your company. I'm afraid both of them were damaged on arrival, so we have a bit of a problem. Are you able to help sort it out for us both?

You could, of course, insert and use the magic 'How...?' word:

? How are you able to help sort this out?

Ask questions using 'softeners'

I mentioned earlier in the book that there are various phrases you can use to introduce a question. The aim of these is to influence the person you are dealing with so that they are in the best possible state to give you the response you want.

? I wonder if you can help? I have a bit of a complaint...
? I'm really sorry to have to bother you with a bit of a complaint, and I hate to make a fuss, but...
? I know how busy you are now and how much you probably hate getting complaints, but...
? Do you mind if I make a constructive comment?

Ask 'choice' questions

This is very simple. Having made the other person aware of your complaint or problem, give them a choice of remedies and ask which they prefer. This will focus their mind on one of them. Provided any of the choices are acceptable for you, you can't lose!

? So I'd be happy to accept either a cash refund right now, or, if it's easier for you, an equivalent reduction off a future holiday. Which do you prefer?

Ask a complaint question after some 'positive praise'

Sometimes you might be complaining about just one particular aspect of something, whilst in all other respects you were perfectly satisfied. In such a situation, always preface your complaint question with the positive aspect (or aspects) first. This gets the person you are dealing with into a more receptive frame of mind, and at the same time it positions you as a fair, reasonable and decent customer.

? I bought a number of items from you last week – look, here's the receipt. Most of them are really great, and I am very pleased with them, but there's just this one that has a problem. What can you suggest?

> **?** I must tell you that this restaurant was recommended to me, and the food has been everything I was told. It has been absolutely fantastic! Unfortunately, though, for some reason or other, the service tonight has been incredibly slow. What do you suggest?

Ask a question that helps them see it from your point of view

Let me give you an example based on the restaurant situation above.

> **?** I must tell you that this restaurant was recommended to me, and the food has been everything I was told. It has been absolutely fantastic! Unfortunately, though, for some reason or other, the service tonight has been incredibly slow. Do you think it's unreasonable of me to be disappointed by having to wait an hour for our main course?

Just yesterday I used this technique when I rang the customer services department of a mail-order organization to tell them some goods I had bought had arrived damaged. There was no problem in them giving us a refund, but initially they wanted me to pay for the carrier service to send them back. At least they did until I asked this question:

> **?** Forgive me, I don't want to be a difficult customer, but do you really think it's fair and reasonable that I should have to pay for the privilege of returning goods to you that I can't keep or use because they are broken?

Back came this reply: 'If you put it like that, I suppose not! OK, I'll arrange for a collection at no cost.'

What to 'just ask' if you don't have the proper documentation

Ever had that situation where you've bought some problem goods, but you no longer have the receipt and you get the 'We can't do anything for you if you don't have the receipt' response? Try this:

> **?** I know that is your normal policy, and I can totally understand why, but in this situation do you really need to see the receipt or are you just going to trust me that I did get the goods from you when I said?

This question actually makes things personal. It makes it harder for them to say 'no', and makes it easy for them to say,

'Well, just this once, I'm sure I can make an exception!'

Who else can I speak to?

There may well be times when you don't get what you want out of a complaint. In these sort of situations ask:

? Well in that case, who else can I speak to?

Questions to 'just ask' yourself if you are on the receiving end of a complaint

? If I were in the customer's situation, how would I feel?

Once you ask yourself this question and focus on your internal response, you are much more likely to deal with the complaint effectively.

? What is my purpose in dealing with this complaint?

I know from experience that there are many people who work in customer services who will automatically think of the professional complainers – the 'moaners' who are after full holiday refunds and compensation because they didn't like the curtains in the bedroom or the uniform the hotel receptionist was wearing. I can tell you, however, having researched this area and advised major companies on their complaints-handling function, that such people are very much in the minority. Here is the stark truth for those of you on the receiving end of complaints: the majority of people who complain *will have* a genuine reason, or else will perceive that they do.

Either way, you, as the person who deals with it, have a problem. The question to ask yourself, then, is **'What is my objective?'** Is it to get rid of the complainer as quickly as possible? Is it to make them feel better? Is your aim to seek to rectify the problem so that they return as a future customer, or to deter them from ever dealing with you again?

In terms of your objectives as a complaints handler, valid questions might also be:

? Even if they are in the wrong, is it in our best interest as a company to perhaps just let them be 'right'?
? Should I just let them tell their story?

One of the things that people who complain want is simply to express their views. Letting them get their problem off their chest will often be the best thing you can do. Ask yourself whether you do this? If not, 'hear them out!'

Questions to ask a person who is complaining

? What exactly would you like me to do about it?

This is a really powerful question to ask, but it must be asked sincerely, politely and prefaced with an apology for something. For example:

? Oh! I'm really sorry to hear that you think we have let you down/ are disappointed / are feeling upset. What can we do to make things up to you?

Why is this such an effective question? Because, as mentioned earlier, many people have not addressed this issue for themselves. Consequently, when you ask it, they are so taken aback by this kind of response that you gain the strategic advantage and control. Notice, too, that the question does not admit any fault on your company's part.

Another good option is to ask 'choice' questions. This is the reverse of the scenario I mentioned earlier. Whatever the problem, consider asking them which of a number of choices would be best for them. For example:

? Oh! I'm really sorry to hear that you're disappointed with the service this evening. If we were to offer you either a 50% reduction off tonight's meal or a voucher for a free meal in the future as a goodwill gesture, which would you prefer?

The important thing to remember is, if you should find yourself on either side of a complaints situation, use questions as a way of dealing with it!

THE POWER OF QUESTIONS – IT'S ALL YOURS!

As we approach the final pages of this book, let me ask you again the question I began with.

? Do you know what holds you back more than anything else?

By now you *do* know the answer.

What holds you back is your failure to JUST ASK for what you want.

You are now in a different place, however. You know the **Golden Rules of 'Just Asking'** and have absorbed the **'Just Asking' mindset**. You have read about the almost miraculous results that can occur when you apply some of the techniques I have explained, and you are now armed with some powerful and provocative questions to ask yourself.

How does all this help?

However simple it seems, 'just asking' is the most influential, life-changing personal tool. Asking the right question, in the right way and at the right time, has huge potential to change the way both you and the person you are asking think, feel and react, and gives you as much control over your own destiny as is humanly possible.

Questions have the power to make you more receptive to new possibilities, fresh ideas and challenges and to help drive you on to – believe it or not – the next question. It is this constant questioning process, which we go through every moment of our lives, that affects our day-to-day focus and, indeed, our overall general state of being.

So what now? How does all I have said help you get what you want?

These are of course questions only *you* can answer or, more importantly, these are the questions *you* need to ask!

Over the years, I have used these rules and techniques myself, and also helped thousands of people in both their personal and business lives to make things happen for themselves, to get closer to their own personal goals, and to make confident decisions with greater peace of mind.

So let me ask you again – now that you have the tools and the mindset,

? What are you going to do now?

You could put this book back on the shelf and forget about what you have just read. The risk, however, is that things will simply stay as they are.

Alternatively, you can actively choose to take the next step and 'just ask' as often as you can, using all the new techniques at your disposal, in order to get closer to what you want.

? Which is it to be?

You now have the power of questions.
When are you going to start to use it?

It will open many new doors for you.
Use it wisely!